THE PHENOMENOLOGY OF DANCE

THE UNIVERSITY

OF WISCONSIN PRESS

MADISON AND

MILWAUKEE 1966

MAXINE SHEETS

THE PHENOMENOLOGY OF dance

Published by
The University of Wisconsin Press
Madison and Milwaukee
P.O. Box 1379
Madison, Wisconsin 53701
Copyright © 1966 by
the Regents of
the University of Wisconsin
Printed in
the United States of America
by Kingsport Press, Inc., Kingsport, Tennessee
Library of Congress
Catalog Card Number 65-24190

TO MILTON M. LOESERMAN

WHO WAS FOR OTHERS AS HE WAS FOR HIMSELF

FOREWORD

Dance is movement, and its opposite, in time and space. It is this continuously changing fact that gives its structure—its permanence in fluidity—and provides a fascination that impels a good many people to be concerned with it: choreographers, performers, teachers, and spectators.

It is its own necessity, not so much as a representation of the moving world, rather as a part of it, with inherent springs.

Mrs. Sheets has chosen here to involve herself with just that aspect of the art that makes up its life and primal force—its moving phenomena—and that, in turn, allows us to have a look into the constant energies.

In a time when many of the college and university dance departments over the United States are dealing with the possibility of including a more direct professional training, Mrs. Sheets' remarks about the arrival of professional dancers on the academic scene as teachers and as professional workers, and the ensuing exchange with the educators, are pertinent.

The continuing aliveness of dance in any situation lies in the individual dancer's solution to the persistent and elusive daily quest for its instant-by-instant behavior, and Mrs. Sheets is pointing out that to look directly at this is a way for the dance in the academic situation to further its already strong and historical achievement.

MERCE CUNNINGHAM

New York
July 17, 1965

ACKNOWLEDGMENTS

The expression of gratitude is not so much a gesture of courtesy as it is a keenly felt affirmation of fact: that this book could not have been written without the generous counsel of several individuals. Since the main text of this book was originally a doctoral dissertation, I am pleased to mention first those people who supervised its writing, especially and most prominently, Mr. Eugene F. Kaelin, Associate Professor of Philosophy at the University of Wisconsin. Without his critical insight and encouragement, the direction and scope of the original descriptive study would not have been realized.

Gratitude is likewise expressed to Miss Louise Kloepper, Associate Professor of Dance at the University of Wisconsin, whose critical reading of the original text was most helpful; especially her suggestions relating to further examples which might assist the reader in grasping the significance of the structures described.

To Mr. James Pratt, Miss Maja Schade, and Miss Muriel Sloan, all of whom served on the doctoral dissertation committee, a second note of thanks is given.

Apart from, yet surrounding and supporting this counsel—as well as the present writing—are three people who either in spirit or directly have had a great deal to do with its realization: Ruth B. Glassow, whose stature as a teacher is exceeded only by her stature as a person; Leigh M. Roberts, through whom the possibility of being and doing became a meaningful reality; and Stanley E. Sheets, my husband, who not only allowed me the freedom to write this book amidst family obligations, but whose patience and faith are immeasurable.

M. S.

Northridge, California
January, 1965

CONTENTS

THE PHENOMENOLOGY OF DANCE

CHAPTER I
PERSPECTIVE

When we look at a dance, what do we see? As choreographers and dancers in the studio and on the stage, what are we creating?

Questions concerning the nature of our experience of dance, and the nature of dance as a formed and performed art, can be provocative and acutely significant. To explore these questions is not only to seek a more informed approach to the teaching of dance, to dance appreciation, to dance criticism, or to choreography; it is also to celebrate, if you will, the uniqueness and vitality of dance in our immediate encounter with it, both as dancers and as audience. When a dance is *there* for us, we intuitively know that it is there; something alive and vibrant is happening on the stage, and as we are totally engaged in our experience of that happening, we too are alive and vibrant: we have a *lived experience*. Judgments, beliefs, interpretations are suspended: our experience of the dance is free of any manner of reflection. We are spontaneously and wholly intent upon the continuously emerging form which appears before us, thoroughly engrossed in its unfolding.

Whatever knowledge we may have of dance, in general or in particular, is extraneous to the lived experience of any dance. Such knowledge may only affect our aesthetic expectations and judgments of that experience. Hence, the kinds of dances we have seen before, the extent of our own participation in dance—all prior experiences with dance influence the manner in which, and the level at which we approach and evaluate it. But to be pre-reflectively involved in what is now appearing before us on the stage is to be fully and exclusively responsive to it, such that the sense of that appearance is immediately and directly apprehended.

The meaning of any dance comes alive for us only as we ourselves have a lived experience of the dance, and is not the result of either prior knowledge of dance or of any later reflective efforts. If we reflect upon the dance after it has been presented in the hope of discovering its meaning, we can only arrive at its significance from a distance. Such a meaning is akin to a lifeless fact, a second-hand piece of information, devoid of felt, lived-through significance. No more than the dance itself, has the meaning truly existed for us. Yet subsequent reflections may encourage us to apprehend in our next experience of the same dance, or in future experiences of dance, something which we have heretofore missed; they may, in fact, rid us of our preconceptions of dance so that our subsequent encounters are immediately and directly meaningful.

It is the lived experience which is of paramount significance. Through the lived experience we arrive not only at the sense of any particular dance, but also at the essence of dance. What is dance? How does it appear? What are the structures inherent in that appearance? Whatever we know of dance and whatever we

may seek to know, it is the immediate encounter which constitutes the foundation of our knowledge: neither dance nor the
lived experience of dance exists apart from the creation and
presentation of the concrete thing itself. What is written down
as a notation of dance is a guide to the future appearance of a
dance, an appearance which is not, until the dance is re-created.
Once it has been re-created and presented, both the dance and
the lived experience of the dance are part of a past which is no
longer. Because what appears before us and what we are immediately aware of are contemporaneous, they point toward an
elucidation of the same phenomenon; it is only the original
emphasis which is different.

If, in the very asking of these questions, we presuppose
nothing in advance, our perspective remains continually fresh
and open, an uncharted and exciting path of discovery. What
emerges is a descriptive analysis and not a body of definitive
knowledge. Answers in the form of definitive knowledge tend
often to become static and sterile because their very patness
estranges them from the thing in question. On the contrary, if
the descriptive analysis is sound and valid, it should continue to
stimulate many vital questions and not dissolve into easy verbal-
isms which lose their significant, felt meaning.

Through the lived experience we discover that dance is first
and foremost a *created* phenomenon: it is a created phenomenon which is presented and which appears before us, a created
phenomenon which we experience. Just as there is no way of
evaluating, much less describing, dance before the experience of
dance is had, so the experience cannot be had before a dance
exists to be experienced. What then is the nature of the created
phenomenon we call dance?

To create a dance is to create a uniquely dynamic form. There
is nothing in any one dance which exists prior to its unique
creation; whatever may constitute the nature of, and structures
inherent in dance, both are created and created anew with each
dance. Moreover, each dance is a complete and unified phenom-

enon, a thoroughly cohesive and continuous form. To arrive at the creation of such a form, the choreographer and dancers are ultimately aware of nothing but the pure dynamics of the total form. They have a lived experience of the sheer dynamic flow of force which is the dance. The created form comes alive in all its rich fullness only as the dancers are reflectively aware neither of themselves, nor of the dance as a pre-existing form through which they move. The dance comes alive precisely as the dancers are *implicitly* aware of themselves and the form, such that the form moves through them: they are not agents of the form, but its moving center. Because they are themselves immersed in what they are creating, because they are not going through specified movements as one would go through a series of technical manoeuvres, what is created and what appears is a unique interplay of fluid, ever-changing forces, a dynamic and cohesive flow of energy, not in the sense that the dancers continually change relationships and positions, but because the dancers and the dance are one.

Apart from the aesthetic grounds upon which one might question the inherent wholeness of any given dance, it is the lived experience of the dance, as it is created and presented, which makes it a unified and continuous whole. So long as we, as dancers and as audience, are wholly and unequivocally engrossed in the dance, the unity and continuity of the work is unbroken. It is only when we reflect upon the experience of the work as it is being created and presented, when we remove ourselves from our immediate encounter with it, that we interrupt the flow and fragmentize its inherent totality. Such reflection ends by obscuring the meaning of the dance, for the meaning emerges only as there is a lived experience of it; only in apprehending the dance in its totality do we discover its unique significance.

The experience must be had *in toto* before any reflection can be meaningful and valid. When judgments, views, or interpretations are meaningful and valid, they can increase the acuity and perspicuity of our aesthetic understanding. Thus, an ever-changing manner in which, and level at which, we approach and evaluate dance. Thus also, a more informed appreciation and criticism. So long as its point of departure is the full, lived experience of dance, reflection can lead to a richer, more vivid and comprehensive understanding of dance. As noted earlier, it may afford the audience of dance a way of discovering new aspects within any given work; hence, it may provide both a sounder and a broader basis for an appreciation and criticism of dance. For choreographers and dancers, reflection may afford insight into approaches to choreography, a deeper under-standing of what it means to create and perform dance, perhaps a growing ability to create dance, and to develop as dancers. For educators in dance, reflection affords the opportunity of an on-going study of dance to discover more meaningful ways of teaching, to the end that they convey to the students, in more and more enlightened ways, both what is involved in, and what preparation is necessary for, the creation and presentation of dance.

The questions posed earlier—What is dance? How does it appear? What are the structures inherent in that appearance?—are questions of immanent concern to those immersed in the making of dances, and to audiences, teachers, and critics. Regardless of his relationship to dance, each forges a conception, a "philosophy," based upon his experience of dance, and through this philosophy he seeks to increase his understanding of the experience, and to utilize that understanding in an increasingly informed approach to creation, instruction, appreciation, and criticism. Yet, it is only by going back to the immediate encounter with dance, again and again, in the studio where dances are created and on the theater stage where they are presented, that one can continue to corroborate his conception of dance and consequently make his approach to any phase of dance an ever more lucid one. Without this corroboration, the conception can be nothing more than a rootless speculation, and the approach has every possibility of becoming nothing more than a self-deluding affectation.

In the same way, it is only by returning to the lived experience of dance that one can begin to discover its uniqueness and vitality. To discover the essence of dance, one must go back repeatedly to the global phenomenon itself, to the indivisible wholeness of any created form. To speak of an indivisible wholeness does not mean that the created form cannot be analyzed. It means only that what is in and of itself complete, a totality, cannot be reduced to a set of elements, parts, or units, for there is no way of reconstituting these separate units into the whole. What is therefore essential to any descriptive analysis of dance is an approach which will not shatter the totality of dance into externally related units, but focus again and again upon the wholeness of the work. Thus we open the door to a phenomenological approach to dance.

To approach dance as a phenomenal presence is to presuppose nothing in advance of the immediate experience of dance. Because nothing is taken for granted, dance is looked upon as a totality whose structures are intrinsic to it. To discover just what this global phenomenon is, constitutes the main project of this book. Such a project is, of course, twofold: to illuminate the nature of, and structures inherent in, the phenomenal presence of dance, and, on the basis of that phenomenal presence, to illuminate the vital immediate encounter with dance as both a formed and performed art. One of the promising features of a phenomenological approach to dance is therefore the possibility of bringing movement and philosophy, creation, performance, and criticism into some kind of meaningful relationship, a relationship whose implications for education in dance may emerge as noteworthy contributions. Hence, a further project is to consider how the phenomenology of dance relates to the teaching of dance, and to determine the place and value of dance within an academic setting.

The first task will be to elucidate the general nature and distinguishing features of phenomenology. Through a more detailed understanding of phenomenology and what constitutes a phenomenological approach, it will be possible to specify more exactly how phenomenology relates to a descriptive study of dance, what is significant in a phenomenological approach to dance, and why a phenomenological approach is potentially meaningful in terms of education in dance.

CHAPTER II
PHENOMENOLOGY:
AN APPROACH
TO DANCE

Phenomenology has to do with descriptions of man and the world, not as objectively constituted, not as given structures which we seek to know through controlled studies or experiments, through observable and recordable patterns of behavior, nor yet through a logical analysis or synthesis of known elements. It has to do rather with descriptions of man and the world as man lives in-the-midst-of-the-world, as he experiences himself and the world, keenly and acutely, before any kind of reflection whatsoever takes place. Its concern is with "foundations," as Husserl, the first to propound the method, described this pre-reflective, pre-objective encounter. Instead of reflecting upon experience as the objective relationship of man to the world, the phenomenologist seeks the heart of the experience itself: the immediate and direct consciousness of man in the face of the world. Instead of taking man and the world for granted, each of which is constituted apart from a relationship to the other, and assuming the reflected-upon experience to be the fundamental interaction of man with his environment, the phenomenologist's approach is rather to describe the foundation or structures of consciousness and the foundation or structuring of the world on the basis of that consciousness. There is an experience, and the experience must be had in order to be described; the trick is to develop a method of description which takes nothing for granted, and which does not falsify or reduce the effect of the experience itself.

Whether "experience" or any other term constitutes the key to theoretical systems, such systems can only offer a reflection on a reflection. And a reflective judgment of whatever nature—empirical, scientific, logical—upon what has already been constituted as a given—the objective reality of man and the objective reality of the world—is a judgment that in part begs the question at issue in *creative* dance. What constitutes the point of departure for theoretical systems is what constitutes the point of arrival for phenomenology: phenomenologically, the "objectively" given has its roots in the human consciousness, as that consciousness intends, or creates its own objects.

Phenomenology is not a theoretical system, and insofar as it could be associated with a system at all, it would probably be described as "existential" analysis. The intended distinction is between a system which reflects upon what the man-world relationship is as the convergence of two objective units, and a systematic method which illuminates the lived experiences of man in-the-midst-of-the-world. No actual theory emerges from phenomenology because phenomenology is concerned not with theories about phenomena, but with descriptions of their existence, which is simply the fact that they appear to consciousness. The resultant description is therefore of a phenomenal presence to consciousness. Fundamentally, man is not an objective structure to be known, but a unique existential being, a unity of consciousness-body, which itself knows. Consequently, any conception of man's relationship to the world must be based upon knowledge of his consciousness-body in a *living* context with the world. Phenomenology is hence more method than system, for it engenders a particular point of view rather than a fixed body of beliefs.

For the phenomenologist, any quest for knowledge about a phenomenon begins with the direct intuition of the phenomenon, apart from any prejudice, expectation, or reflection; hence, this direct intuition is *pre-reflective*. The phenomenologist's attitude toward the phenomenon is neither objective nor subjective, but rather an attitude of being present to the phenomenon, fully and wholly, to intuit it as it appears, without preshaping it in any way by prior interpretations or beliefs. He is thus led to describe the "lived experience" of the phenomenon, the essential relationship between consciousness and its world. Through his description of the lived experience, he is able to elucidate *structures* apparent in the phenomenon, forms existing within the total form of life. Thus, if dance is the phenomenon, the phenomenologist describes the immediate encounter with dance, the lived experience of dance, and proceeds from there to describe the analyzable structures, such as temporality and spatiality, inherent in the total experience.

Since the phenomenon is described as it gives itself to consciousness, it is apparent that the phenomenologist looks upon the something happening as an appearance of something, an appearance which indubitably is. Regardless of whether the why or how of the appearance may be factually explained, the fact that something does appear and does exist cannot be called into question. If something appears to consciousness, it is furthermore evident that consciousness is consciousness of something; that is, every consciousness intends an object and is not merely a blind receiver of impressions. The phenomenon gives itself to consciousness only as consciousness is conscious of it, only as there is an immediate, pre-reflective, intuitional awareness. As such, the lived experience engenders a meaning of some order. The pre-reflective, pre-judicative consciousness is not a passive container of impressions, but a consciousness of felt significance, import, or meaning.

The phenomenological method is one of description; yet, as is evident, it is at the same time more than that, for in aiming toward a description of the phenomenon, it reflects backwards toward an elucidation of the structures of consciousness. It by-passes all question of the subject's objectivity or the object's subjectivity by elucidating the immediate world of lived experience, the world as it is immediately and directly known through a pre-reflective consciousness. This initial and direct knowledge constitutes the foundation upon which all future knowledge is built.

Through the foregoing description of phenomenology, we may begin to see how phenomenology relates to a descriptive study of dance. Dance is a phenomenon: it, too, gives itself to consciousness; it appears, and the consciousness of dance is a pre-reflective consciousness. Yet beyond this, it is clear that dance is a particular kind of phenomenon, namely, one which moves, one which is kinetic. A descriptive study of dance must therefore concern itself with an appearance, a phenomenon, which, while moving, remains a totality.

In order to explicate the kinetic nature of the phenomenon of dance, we will pursue the exposition of phenomenology further by describing the phenomenological constructs of two structures which exist within the total lived experience of any kinetic phenomenon: time and space. There are several reasons why such an excursion is both desirable and pertinent. A description of these structures will, of course, illustrate concretely the nature of a phenomenological analysis. But equally, if not more importantly, such a description will provide the foundation for an understanding of how the temporality and spatiality of dance are structures inherent in the kinetic phenomenon of dance itself; and further, how a new terminological-conceptual framework is necessarily generated to describe both the kinetic phenomenon of dance and the lived experience of that phenomenon.

To elaborate on these latter two benefits, it may first be noted that the question, What is dance? has certainly been answered before from an historical, scientific, and educational point of view. The concern here, however, is not with the series of events called dance which have occurred through the ages, with the series of events which are objective correlates of a moving body, nor with the ways in which dance as part of an educational curriculum meets educational standards. The focal point of concern here is precisely that elusive moving form which is created and which appears before us on the stage: the dance as both a formed and performed art. A phenomenological account of time and space as structures within the total lived experience of any kinetic phenomenon, will provide the foundation of our understanding of how these structures are integral parts of that elusive moving form.

It may also be noted that the empirical answer which is sometimes given to the question, What is dance? namely, that dance is a force in time and space, is not descriptive of the *lived experience* of dance. When we see a dance, we do not see separate objective factors with no unifying center. What we see is something which perhaps can only be empirically written as forcetimespace; an indivisible wholeness appears before us. Space, time, and force are certainly apparent in dance, but they are not and cannot be objectively apparent. To conceive of them as given objective factors beforehand is to overlook the very quiddity of dance: it is something which is created and which does not exist prior to its creation.

In reference to how a new terminological-conceptual framework is generated, it is evident that if one follows the phenomenological method, one sometimes discovers, within the total structure of the thing presented, new insight into the nature of its appearance. This insight, in turn, leads to new descriptions, and thus sometimes to a new terminology. It is readily apparent that the concepts thus engendered emanate from the primary encounter with the thing in question. In other words, there is first the appearance of the thing, that is, a dance, and secondly the conceptual framework which is built up in describing it. The new concepts—new only in terms of their being related to dance—which will be presented within the following phenomenological accounts of time and space, are essential to an understanding of dance. They are neither vapid academic reflections upon dance, nor are they concepts which must be artificially grafted onto it; rather, they are descriptive of its immediate phenomenal presence. Specifically, they describe the nature of form in dance, both as it is created and presented. Hence, these new concepts are to be taken neither as intellectual stuffing nor as metaphysical glorifications of dance: they describe the lived experience itself. If the purpose is to elucidate the nature of dance and the structures inherent in dance, then hopefully, the fullness of the lived experience of dance, an experience which we know, should be enriched rather than dessicated by the analysis.

According to recent phenomenologists, temporality and spatiality are inherent structures of human consciousness-body. They are rooted in man's foundational pre-reflective awareness of himself, and not in the more abstractly refined notions of "real" time and "real" space: the immediate lived experience of time and space is epistemologically prior to our notions of objective time and objective space. The specific descriptions which follow are based upon the writings of two eminent and articulate phenomenologists, Jean-Paul Sartre [1] and Maurice Merleau-Ponty.[2] Sartre has elucidated the phenomenological nature of time in his book, *Being and Nothingness*. He has, of

1. Jean-Paul Sartre, *Being and Nothingness*, trans. Hazel Barnes (New York, 1956), pp. 107–70, 204–16.
2. Maurice Merleau-Ponty, *Phénoménologie de la Perception* (Paris, 1945), pp. 81–179; Eugene F. Kaelin, *An Existentialist Aesthetic* (Madison, Wisconsin, 1962), pp. 230–49.

course, been heavily influenced by Martin Heidegger.[3] Merleau-Ponty has written extensively on the phenomenological nature of space, centering his phenomenology of perception and behavior on the spatial presence of human consciousness-body. The phenomenological construct of time describes a complete totality whose sub-structures, past, present, and future, form distinct but interrelated units. Their interrelationship is internally rather than externally defined: they do not exist as an isolated series of "nows," but as sub-structures whose meaning derives from their being intrinsic to the whole. If past, present, and future were externally related, their meaning as a disconnected series of "nows," a series of given moments, would be nowhere, for the past was never present and the future will never become present; their non-presence cancels their meaning. Similarly, the present, as an infinitesimal point or "now," is a moment so instantaneous that its meaning is impossible to grasp. Past, present, and future constitute temporality as an *internally* related synthesis whose foundation is within human consciousness-body. Objective time, measurable durations and tempos, is constituted upon this existential foundation. In order to understand how foundational temporality is decomposed into objective time, the nature of original or foundational temporality must first be described.

Original temporality is founded upon the *ekstatic*[4] structure of human consciousness-body. Man does not *have* a past since he *is* his past in the mode of not being it; he is always already present. He does not *have* a present, but *is* his present in the mode of not being fixed in the instant: his present is a flight which projects him into his future. Finally, he does not *have* a future since he *is* his future in the mode of not being it; his

3. Edith Kern, ed., *Sartre: A Collection of Critical Essays* (Englewood Cliffs, New Jersey: Prentice-Hall, 1962), pp. 5–13; Martin Heidegger, *Being and Time*, trans. J. Macquarrie and E. Robinson (London: Student Christian Movement Press, 1962).

4. The three temporal dimensions—past, present, future—are described in terms of the three ways man's being stands out (*ek-stasis*) from itself.

future is not yet, but is outlined upon the present out of which he moves toward the future as to a goal. Man comprises temporality within himself, for he is such an *ekstatic* being: he is always at a distance from himself, always in flight. Man negates himself as being past, present, or future while at the same time he apprehends himself as being that temporal totality. He can never apprehend himself as a complete temporal being, existing fully in any given moment, without making himself into an object. Man's apprehension of himself as a temporal totality is a pre-reflective awareness of himself in-the-midst-of-the-world. Hence, consciousness is not explicitly consciousness of itself as it lives, nor of its *ekstatic* structure; such explicit awareness would constitute a reflection upon the lived experience of consciousness. Temporality is founded upon man's pre-reflective awareness of himself as he lives; man only *implicitly* cognizes himself as *ekstatic*, and then only in experiential form.

We may illustrate this implicit awareness of self in the context of everyday life. In crossing a street, a person is neither explicitly aware of himself nor of his *ekstatic* structure: he constitutes himself neither as an object nor as being, fully and wholly, at any one moment, as he crosses the street. He is implicitly aware of himself and his *ekstatic* dimensions, implicitly aware of himself as realizing his intention: "to cross the street." If he were explicitly aware of himself in the act of crossing, he would constitute and apprehend himself as an object, and he would be conscious of himself as transporting this object self at every moment, from "this present now," to "this present now," ad infinitum: and these present "nows" would have no internal relationship. Each step forward would be apprehended as a discrete "now," and the person would be explicitly aware of himself as being that discrete "now" every step of the way. On the contrary, as the lived experience which it usually is, crossing the street is an intentional act which is all of a piece: because it is the "theme" of consciousness, it is a temporal totality. The person crossing the street is implicitly aware of himself as past-present-future, in the mode of not being any one of these at any given moment. The temporal flight of his being is implicitly apprehended in the very act of crossing, which exists for him not as a segmented series of steps but as a totality. The synthesized yet unachieved totality of past, present, and future, which is original temporality, thus exists because human consciousness exists; it is at the foundation a basic structure of the being of human consciousness.

Within the total structure of original temporality are two substructures: static temporality and dynamic temporality. In being implicitly aware of his temporality, man may pre-reflectively apprehend that temporality as a flow from past to future, or from future to past. In static temporality, each instant is apprehended as a separate unit, an independent unit of the succession "before," "now," "after," from past to future. If a temporal flow is to be re-established so that there is unity in such multiplicity, there again must be an internal rather than external relationship between the units. The units are internally related because human consciousness, in its *ekstatic* dimensions, is at the same time a multiple unity and a unified multiplicity. Multiplicity and unity coexist because human consciousness exists as a temporal multiplicity (past, present, future) and a temporal unity (the synthesis of these units). Temporality is thus *diasporatic*: while it is a single cohesive structure, it is a structure whose meaning derives only from the interrelationship of its units. Because human consciousness exists diasporatically, as a temporal cohesion and temporal dispersion of its being, static temporality is likewise diasporatic: it exists both as a multiple unity and a unified multiplicity.

The second sub-structure of original temporality, dynamic temporality, is a pre-reflective awareness of the flow of time from future to past. We may illustrate this implicit awareness of temporal flow from future to past in the context of everyday life, for any intentional act characterized by an expectant consciousness is a lived experience of temporality from future to past. A person is then implicitly aware of himself as surpassing himself toward his past rather than toward his future. The intentional act may not be "to cross the street" but "to be on the other side"; thus, temporality is lived in reverse to "historical time." The intention, "to be on the other side," is a future which the person "is" only insofar as he surpasses his present and past. The person implicitly apprehends the temporal totality of his being as a backward flow: each step forward is temporally a step backward toward the past until the person reaches his future, until he realizes his intention, "to be on the other side." But the future is no longer the moment it becomes present, that is, the moment the person "is" on the other side. As Sartre has noted, "what I was waiting for—here it is." [5]

Human consciousness attains a permanency in this "backward flow" because it endures as a being perpetually in flight. Just as man never succeeds in overcoming his temporal distance from himself, in effacing the nothingness which separates him from his goal, so he never succeeds in achieving himself as a temporal totality: he is always surpassing the instant as he surpasses himself toward his past. He endures precisely because he never is, completely and wholly, at any given instant.

The reflection which apprehends static or dynamic temporality is a reflection of human consciousness as a unity of succession or as an enduring consciousness, but never a self as object. In such an act of pure reflection, man is at the same time both witness and appearance to himself, both the reflecting consciousness and the consciousness reflected upon. Through such reflection, human consciousness looks for and attempts to found its being, its totality which is always in flight; but such reflection is never wholly successful, because consciousness can neither be totally the reflecting consciousness without its object, nor can it

5. Sartre, *Being and Nothingness*, p. 145.

detach itself in order to take a point of view on itself. Pure reflection therefore constitutes immediate knowledge without revelation, for no given emanates from the reflection.

In sum, original temporality is a fundamental structure of human consciousness-body, a structure of which we are implicitly aware until that precise moment in which we reflect upon ourselves as an object. At that precise moment, either the unity of succession, which is static temporality, or the enduring consciousness, which is dynamic temporality, is no longer implicitly apparent. What is apparent is the self as object, a "self-conscious" complete temporal given at every moment. Hence, we move from original temporality to psychic temporality.

Psychic temporality reveals consciousness as a successive order of facts: actions, states, and qualities which are externally linked to one another. Each psychic fact becomes a thing in itself, an appearance, such that human consciousness loses its *ekstatic* structure and becomes a succession of externally related "nows." Since consciousness makes itself into an object and accepts itself as such, any psychic fact presents itself as an objective rather than a lived reality. For example, "I *am* sad." Because I constitute myself as being a given thing in the given moment, temporality dissolves into a series of qualitative befores and afters which are externally unified, and objective time is thereby constituted. It may be noted that deterministic psychologies which outline the history of a person as the sum and sequence of his psychic states and actions are founded upon psychic temporality.

Finally, objective temporality is not only an objectification of self; it is also an objectification of the world by human consciousness, but again, on the foundation of its own original temporality. Man confers temporal values upon objects in the world which would otherwise be atemporal. Human consciousness in its own *ekstatic* dimensions apprehends objects as enduring, complete in their past, present, and future. As Sartre has so gracefully put it, the object transcends the time which flows over it,[6] for it is indifferent to the multiplicity of its appearances which are externally related to one another in time by human consciousness. Objective temporality is, then, a container of all *externally related appearances*. It is made to be by human consciousness which enforces a cohesion upon separate and otherwise atemporal instants. If the object's past were uncreated, it would have no meaning as an appearance in the present because its present would not be apprehended as a present, nor would the future possibilities of its appearances be apprehended as a future. Man organizes time by compressing into blocks of time the separate and dispersed instants in which the object appears. And the object remains totally indifferent to the imposed temporality.

From this brief description of temporality, it is apparent that time exists because human consciousness exists, and it has become clear how temporality is an inherent structure of human consciousness. Our consciousness of time emanates from the immediate awareness we have of our own synthesized yet never achieved totality: my past is yesterday only because I am immediately aware of my presence today and my future tomorrow. Night follows day as an objective temporal succession only because consciousness relates the regular appearances of light and darkness into a meaningful temporal relationship. Consciousness endows the world with a unified temporal structure by relating appearances which are external to one another. But it constitutes this objective time on the basis of its own original temporality.

A pre-reflective awareness of time is thus intrinsic to any lived experience of consciousness-body, for example, crossing a street, kicking a football, waving goodbye; thus, it is intrinsic also to the dancer's lived experience of the dance. A dance, as it is formed and performed, is experienced by the dancer as a perpetually moving form, a unity of succession, whose moments cannot be

6. Sartre, *Being and Nothingness*, p. 205.

measured: its past has been created, its present is being created, its future awaits creation. Yet, it is not an externally related series of pasts, presents, futures—befores, nows, and afters; it is truly *ekstatic*, it is in flight, it is in the process of becoming the dance which it is, yet is never the dance at any moment. The dance at any moment is diasporatic, a perpetually moving form whose "moments" are all of a piece.

Just as objective time is founded upon the original temporality of consciousness-body, so objective space is founded upon the original spatiality of consciousness-body. Man in-the-midst-of-the-world is able to endow the world with an objective spatial structure because he is already implicitly aware of himself as a unity of consciousness-body which is spatially present. The unity of consciousness-body, never the object self, but the *lived* self, is nowhere more apparent than in the immediacy and directness with which consciousness "exists" [7] its body as its spatial presence. Its "hereness" is the existential foundation upon which objective space, measurable distances and relationships, is constituted. Again, we must begin by describing the nature of the foundational structure of human consciousness-body in order to understand how it is decomposed; how a lived reality is dissolved into an objective reality.

Any lived experience of the body incorporates a pre-reflective awareness of its spatiality through the bodily schema. Consciousness-body knows itself to be spatially present in-the-midst-of-the-world, not through a factual kinesthetic perception of its parts, but through a pre-reflective awareness of itself as a spatially present totality. To apprehend the totality of the body is to live the body and not to reflect upon it as a given object or

7. The verb "exist" is used transitively in the writings of contemporary phenomenologists. The closest synonym is "live": consciousness "exists" or "lives" its body as the inescapable contingency of its being; ". . . the relation of consciousness to the body is an *existential* relation." (Sartre, *Being and Nothingness*, p. 329.) This usage and meaning will be followed in the whole of the text and will be clarified specifically in relation to dance in Chapter III.

as the sum and sequence of kinesthetic sensations. The body's "hereness" is a totality, and not an externally related system of parts. Its "hereness" as a spatial totality, however, is not an isolated and static series of spatial moments, an implicit awareness of "being here," and "being here," and "being here," but rather, a continuous and unified "being hereness": the bodily gestures and movements which are lived kinetic experiences of consciousness-body's spatial presence.

The bodily schema is the foundation of the pre-reflective knowledge of the body's spatiality; it synthesizes all spatial presences of the body. It is, in fact, the bodily schema which allows us to grasp our gestures and movements as a continuous and unified "being hereness." For example, in typing a word, each movement toward a key is not reflected upon separately, nor is all the movement necessary to type the word reflected upon prior to moving. "The corporeal schema . . . summarizes the situation of the body before its tasks";[8] hence, it is a fluid, ever-changing projection of body movement as a *Gestalt*. What is pre-reflectively grasped is not the projected *Gestalt* of body movement, but a knowledge and sense of the body's movements and gestures; the bodily schema does not present us with a projection in the form of an image of our body, but gives us an immediate knowledge and sense of its gestures. In any lived experience, one is neither explicitly aware of bodily movements as a discrete series of parts nor as the sum of a series of parts. It is not a question of being explicitly aware of bodily sensations as we move and judging our spatial reference points in relation to these sensations, for we are already implicitly aware of our spatiality. Because the sensations are already directly meaningful through the bodily schema, our gestures and movements exist for us as a totality.

Consciousness-body moves out toward the world in which it is already implicitly aware of being spatially present. It extends its

8. Kaelin, *An Existentialist Aesthetic*, p. 239.

spatiality toward the world as a means of relating to and communicating with it. We reach out to shake someone's hand, we throw a ball in the air, we travel by various modes from where we are to some place else; we extend our spatiality through the world and toward or away from any situation in which we implicitly know ourselves to be spatially present. It is therefore clear that in any lived experience, consciousness-body is not explicitly aware of its spatial presence as it moves: such awareness would constitute consciousness-body as an object. In any lived experience, consciousness-body is explicitly aware of whatever it constitutes as its object in-the-midst-of-the-world, and it is implicitly aware of its own spatial presence as the meaning of its gestures in relation to that object. The lived experience of spatiality is thus a lived experience of meaningful gestures.

We may illustrate the lived experience of spatiality in-the-midst-of-the-world in the common, everyday movement of reaching. If I reach for a pen which is on the table, it is because I am pre-reflectively aware of my spatial presence in relation to the pen. My immediate "hereness" carries with it a correlative notion of "thereness." Because I apprehend my body in the environment as a spatial presence, I intuitively know the spatial presence and meaning of things in my environment. Its "thereness" exists for me only because my "hereness" exists for me. My spatial presence toward the pen is thus a meaning which my body understands in its gesture toward the pen.

We may note, furthermore, that consciousness takes a point of view on the world only because the body establishes a point of view. I am not suddenly aware of a distance separating me from the pen, for the vision of the pen is already a point of view—already an intuited meaning of my spatial presence. Thus, I do not eke out movement from my body, interpreting its point-to-point progress toward the pen as a fulfillment of my efforts to reach it. I reach the pen because my body understands the meaning of objects as that meaning is intended in the act of seeing those objects. To paraphrase Merleau-Ponty, the body extends its spatiality, that is, grasps its objects, "in one swoop of the intentional arc." [9]

Consciousness-body, through its implicit awareness of its spatial presence, constitutes the spatiality of its environment. At the same time, it knows the meaning of that constituted spatiality in its very point of view upon it. Consciousness experiences its world and itself through its body. If we have conscious experiences, it is because our body moves within the environment as a spatial presence and intuitively knows the meaning of its spatiality.

Through the above example, it has undoubtedly become clear that the spatiality of consciousness-body is *ekstatic*. Its "hereness" does not refer to an objective spatial presence, but to a pre-objective presence, and it furthermore refers not to a static body but to a dynamic body. The spatial being of consciousness-body, its inherent spatiality, is no more apprehended as being at a particular place than is its temporal being apprehended as being at a particular moment. In the above example, the spatial presence, the "hereness," is not referable to the body either as object or as static: my "hereness" in relation to the pen is a spatial *ekstasis*, insofar as I do not apprehend myself as being spatially "here," fully and wholly, at any one point in space as I reach for the pen. In short, a spatial as well as temporal *ekstasis* is an inherent foundational structure of the being of human consciousness-body, and the spatial *ekstasis* like the temporal *ekstasis* dissolves only when consciousness-body apprehends itself reflectively as an object. It is at that point as well as at that moment that the spatial totality of consciousness-body is decomposed and consciousness-body becomes a system of externally related parts.

One cannot speak of being at a temporal moment without speaking at the same time of being at a particular place at that moment. Space and time, whether objectively constituted or as

9. Kaelin, *An Existentialist Aesthetic*, p. 253; cf. Merleau-Ponty, *Phénoménologie*, p. 164.

lived, are never actually separate structures. Time does not exist apart from space and space does not exist apart from time; furthermore, both are apprehended in the same way. One cannot be pre-reflectively aware of his temporal totality and at the same time be reflectively aware of himself as a discrete spatial object. Thus, consciousness-body is foundationally not only a spatially and temporally *ekstatic* being, but also a being which is spatially as well as temporally diasporatic. The above example illustrates that the body's moving spatial presence is both a unified multiplicity and a multiple unity: the act of reaching is a projected arc which is a single movement whose particular spatial units characterize the total movement as being this particular movement and none other: I reach the pen without wavering on my course toward it, without over-reaching or under-reaching. Likewise, it is a movement which is uniquely meaningful because each unit within the arc is internally related to all other units: each spatial point, each unit of "being here" and "being here," is unified by the bodily schema, and it is this unification which makes the intentional act of reaching a meaningful gesture—hence, a multiple unity.

In any lived experience, we are always pre-reflectively aware of the spatial-temporal totality of our being because we are never conscious of ourselves as being at any one moment in time or at any one point in space: the spatial-temporal units of our being which constitute our spatial-temporal totality are not explicitly recognized. Because we are implicitly aware of ourselves in any lived experience, we understand the meaning of that lived experience.

Any explicit awareness of the body is perforce an unsuccessful reflection upon the body. The body may never be completely experienced as an object against a background of other objects, because consciousness is able to take a point of view on all things in the world except its own body, which it can only live. When experienced as an incomplete object, the body, from being an ever-changing absolute point of orientation apprehended pre-reflectively, becomes a relative spatial point in the objective world. The reflected-upon body is always an externally related system of parts and never a totality which is lived. As an objective system of parts, the body is often regarded as an instrument of consciousness, an instrument explicitly recognized as carrying out whatever consciousness intends. Such is frequently the situation in learning a new skill, for example, because the body, while it understands the intentional act, is not yet able to coordinate its gestures toward a realization of that act. The skill is had precisely at the point at which the body ceases to be an object manipulated toward a given end and becomes, instead, a lived meaning or a lived experience of meaningful gestures. And it becomes a lived experience of meaningful gestures at the moment the skill is integrated with the bodily schema and one is pre-reflectively aware of his body in the act.

The body's reflective knowledge of itself as an object is the basis upon which objective space is constituted. Insofar as we are reflectively aware of the dimensions of our body as an object, we are aware of the dimensions of other objects in the world. The body becomes a relative point of spatial orientation toward the world and at the same time becomes one object among many objects which are contained in the given space. We circumscribe the given objective space in many ways to correspond to the natural circumscription of our bodies as objects: houses, fences, etc. We make containers within the great objective container and attempt to mark off specific boundaries of ourselves as spatial objects. The body relates to and communicates with the world in extending its spatiality in-the-midst-of-the-world; and in a reverse way, it reflectively asserts itself as a circumscribed object, marking off the limits of its domain and privacy in the objective world. Objective space is thus a container of all things, including consciousness-body, but it is constituted upon the basis of an original spatiality: man's foundational pre-reflective awareness of his own non-objective spatial presence.

A pre-reflective awareness of space is thus also intrinsic to any lived experience of consciousness-body; hence, intrinsic to the dancer's lived experience of the dance. The foregoing descriptions of temporality and spatiality make clear the fact that any lived experience of the body incorporates a pre-reflective grasp of its temporality and spatiality because these structures are inherent in human consciousness-body. They also make clear the fact that the lived experience of the body is a kinetic phenomenon, e.g., crossing the street, reaching for a pen, creating a dance. Yet, as we shall see, whether the kinetic phenomenon is the movement of our own body, or whether it is the movement of something which appears before us, for example, a dance, a lived experience of the phenomenon incorporates a pre-reflective grasp of its temporality and spatiality.

As we are totally engaged in the experience of any kinetic phenomenon, we are implicitly aware of its inherent spatial-temporal structure. Only when we see the kinetic phenomenon as an object which is moving, when we reflect upon it, separate or distance ourselves from it, are its inherent spatiality and temporality decomposed. The phenomenon then becomes for us an object or a thing which moves within a given space and within a given time. In the immediate encounter with the phenomenon, whether it be the flight of a jet across the sky, the stalking of a cat toward its prey, or a dance, what appears before us is a moving form which exists within its own spatial-temporal structure. It is therefore clear that in our lived experience of dance, we are implicitly aware of the spatiality and temporality of the particular moving form which appears before us. The moving form does not subsist within objective time or objective space, but space and time subsist within the totality of the moving form. Space and time are neither appropriated by the dance as dimensions in which it can occur, nor are they appended to our lived experience of the dance. They are integral parts of an integral whole, structures which are inherent in the total phenomenal presence of dance.

The dance, as it is formed and performed by the dancers, is a unity of succession, a cohesive moving form, and so it is to the audience. What appears before us is not an externally related series of spatial-temporal befores, nows, and afters, but a form which is *ekstatic*, in flight, in the process of becoming the dance which it is, yet never fully the dance at any moment. What appears before us is diasporatic, a perpetually moving form whose "moments" are all of a piece. In short, the dance appears as it has been created: a kinetic phenomenon whose spatiality and temporality are structures created with and inherent in the total global phenomenon itself.

If the phenomenological constructs of time and space have been significant in elucidating the foundational spatial-temporal structures inherent in the total lived experience of any kinetic phenomenon, they have also been significant in emphasizing once again the paramount importance of the lived experience itself, specifically the lived experience of dance. Dance is not only a kinetic phenomenon which appears, which gives itself to consciousness; it is also a living, vital human experience as both a formed and performed art: the experience for both dancer and audience is a *lived* experience. Without returning again and again to this lived experience, one cannot hope to arrive at a valid and meaningful description of dance, the nature of, and structures inherent in, its appearance, creation, and presentation. This emphasis upon the immediate, unreflected-upon experience of dance is necessarily vital to all concerned with dance: critics, choreographers, dancers, audiences, teachers. Yet for educators in dance, it is perhaps most essential, since it is their duty to instruct others, to impart to them a deep and comprehensive knowledge of dance, both practical and conceptual. Because others come explicitly to them in order to learn of dance, and because they undoubtedly influence others, the knowledge which they communicate must be based upon an intimate acquaintance with dance as a formed and performed art. The foregoing descriptions are thus meaningful as a point of departure to explore what the educational implications of a phenomenological approach to dance might be.

A phenomenological approach opens the way toward an understanding of how dance as subject matter relates to education. It offers the opportunity of re-evaluating the place of dance in an academic setting by elucidating the nature of dance, to the end that the educational values assigned to it coincide more closely with what it is, or even better, emanate from it. From an educational point of view, dance is sometimes justified in terms of leading to self-realization, individual growth, an appreciation of democratic principles in action, etc. Although the educative potential of dance may certainly include these facets of knowledge, the question may be asked whether such justifications do not exploit dance to the extent that it is no longer an art form, but merely an artistic means to a non-artistic end. It would seem that the problem is to provide an analysis of dance which will elucidate its values for education on the basis of what it is, rather than affix preconstructed educational values upon it. Perhaps other educational values are to be found in dance which might preserve it as an end in itself.

To provide an analysis of dance which might bring to light its intrinsic values for education, one must first answer the question, What is dance? The terms in which the answer is stated will reveal the kind of analysis made, and the kind of analysis made will, in turn, determine the educational values to be found in dance. The tendency, when this question is answered on aesthetic grounds, has been to weight the answer on the side of the dancer (expression of feelings or ideas), on the side of the audience (evocation of feelings or ideas), or to balance both sides equally (communication), without really describing what dance itself is or how it functions, if it does, as a vehicle for expression, evocation, or communication. What is needed is a synthetic view of dance as a formed (dancer point of view) and performed (audience point of view) art. This synthesis is possible through a phenomenological approach to dance, since it perforce recognizes dance as a formed and performed art. Moreover, if there is any question of by-passing the art of dance within an educational curriculum, it may be because dance has been taken out of movement, and the educational value of dance may be quite different from the educational value of movement. That many colleges and universities are bringing in professional dancers may be a tacit recognition that something is lacking in "educational" dance. If a phenomenological approach to dance can clarify the relationship of movement to dance, it can lay the groundwork for the distinction between dance in education and movement education.

Finally, one of the foremost educational values of a phenomenological approach is that it is open-ended. One's description of the thing in question may not only provide the basis upon which other phenomenological studies may be made, but it may also be further elaborated by others whose experience of the thing goes beyond the original description. This elaboration is possible, however, only insofar as others verify the original description by their own lived experiences of the phenomenon in question, dance, both as it is created and as it is presented. What may come of such elaboration is an on-going literature of the dance, an ever-broadening knowledge and appreciation of what it means to create, present, and experience dance. The value of such an on-going literature for education in dance is notably evident, and not only because it is conspicuously missing: at the least, it would provide a much needed arena for discussion, and at the most, a comprehensive, though thoroughly individualized, approach to the art of dance.

CHAPTER III
A PHENOMENOLOGICAL
ACCOUNT OF THE
ILLUSION OF FORCE

In the first chapter, the lived experience of dance was described as an experience of a sheer dynamic flow of force. This account of the dance is actually an elaboration of an original phenomenological description presented by Susanne Langer in her book *Feeling and Form*.[1] In that book Mrs. Langer described dance as creating and presenting an *illusion of force* through a symbolic form. She thus described the immediately grasped phenomenon of dance, the dance as it is immanently present to consciousness. A major assumption of this book is that this description is sound and meaningful. Yet it is not one which anyone is asked to accept uncritically. On the contrary, what is vital is to verify by one's own intuition of dance whether an illusion of force is of

1. Susanne Langer, *Feeling and Form* (New York, 1953).

the essence. Before one can decide this, however, one must know just what Mrs. Langer means by "illusion of force." It will be the purpose of this chapter both to clarify and develop that meaning.

According to Mrs. Langer, art creates a semblance or illusion of reality by a symbolization of that reality. "Illusion" or "semblance" refers to the pure appearance of a thing stripped of its practical function or value. This sheer appearance is what is given and given alone in the immediate experience of a work of art. Such an immediate experience is possible because the art work is created and presented as a symbol, and what it symbolizes is the form of actual human feelings. Although the outward form in which the art work is created is different from everyday forms of feeling, that is, non-discursive rather than discursive, the formal properties of its structure are logically related to the formal properties of actual human feelings. There is an organic similarity in the dynamic structure of the artistic forms and the everyday forms of feeling: tension-release, suspension-fall, anticipation-climax, attenuation-abruptness, etc. The art work is a symbol, for it reveals a logical congruence of form with that which it symbolizes. The primary illusion the art work creates comes to life with the making of the symbol. This, in brief, constitutes Mrs. Langer's conception of art.

In looking at dance and in asking what is created, Mrs. Langer states that *virtual force* is the primary illusion which comes to life with the making of the dance. But dance as the creation of virtual force may be further elucidated in that we can describe the structures of that illusion: its nature and qualities are not hidden essences but apparent ones. It is the nature of the illusion, the foundation of its appearance, and the structures inherent in that appearance which will constitute the specific concern of this chapter.

The phenomenological basis for maintaining that virtual force is the primary illusion of dance is that movement itself is primarily a revelation of force. In dance, the movement of the human body transforms and is experienced as transforming its own material reality so that it is viewed from the beginning as an illusion of force. Such a description of virtual force necessarily involves questions of time and space, for the human body, movement, and therefore virtual force are in some manner related to these dimensions. Mrs. Langer designates these dimensions as secondary illusions. That is, the foremost thing created in dance and the thing which is therefore immediately given to consciousness is virtual force, the primary illusion. What may be given secondarily are the spatial or temporal illusions ". . . which are really devices that support the total creation or enhance its expressiveness." [2] Rather than making a substratum of illusion, one may question whether, on the contrary, the illusion is not itself spatially unified and temporally continuous, for it is phenomenologically as well as logically impossible for virtual force to take place in "real" time and in "real" space without thereby losing its virtuality.

Since an illusion is created from reality and reality from the tangible physical world, we will first look at the spatial-temporal aspects of the human body, the physical reality underlying the primary illusion. It is the human body which, in the creation of that illusion, transcends its material reality to become the source of virtual force and a symbol within the total phenomenon of the dance.

The human body as a physical phenomenon is a singular mass. Its spatial definition is always unitary and indivisible: regardless of the shape it assumes, the area which it displaces can be traced by a single, unbroken line. Since there is no dispersion of parts but a spatial totality, the human body appears existentially unified in space.

The human body is also an enduring mass. Its temporal definition is always continuous and indivisible: regardless of the changes in its appearance, the span of its existence is of an

2. Langer, *Feeling and Form*, p. 205.

unbroken duration. Since it is not temporally dispersed, existing, then not existing, the human body appears existentially continuous in time.

The question therefore is how these physical spatial-temporal definitions, unification and continuity, are related to body movement, to the body's expression of force. A description of the spatial-temporal dimensions, in other words, must necessarily become more complex as the physical mass of the body becomes a center of actual force in daily movement, and as it becomes a center of virtual force in dance.

By virtue of movement, the human body must be considered as something more than a physical structure: its being incorporates consciousness as well as corporeality. Because there is something which feels, wills, and intends bodily actions, it becomes necessary and vital to explore the relationship of consciousness to the body; specifically, the relationship of consciousness to the body in movement, and the spatial-temporal aspects of that relationship. Since a single human being is the foundation for the existence of both consciousness and body, the description of the relationship must necessarily proceed from an ontological basis; that is, with the nature of the reality of movement as it is experienced by any human being.

It is phenomenologically evident that all consciousness is consciousness of something. But as we have seen, in any lived experience, nothing is objectively constituted: neither consciousness itself nor the object of consciousness exists as a given. Thus, in looking at a dance, I implicitly know that I am looking at the dance at the same time that I am totally and experientially involved in seeing it. Similarly, as a dancer, I am implicitly aware of myself as I create the dance. On the pre-reflective level there is no possibility of being "self-conscious" in the sense of apprehending the body as an object. On the pre-reflective level, consciousness can only exist its body as the contingency of its being, as the inescapable structure of its existence. As such, it is the unreflected-upon, lived experience which pinpoints the consciousness-body relationship at the primary ontological level. What we must determine is the nature of this lived experience: How does consciousness exist its body in movement, in dance?

When consciousness exists its body in movement, it does so as an immediate pre-reflective consciousness of a form being made, a form moving toward completion, never totally present at any single instant or point. Since movement is never complete at any one instant or point, never fully there, consciousness exists its body in movement as a form continuously projecting itself toward a spatial-temporal future; hence, as a *form-in-the-making*. This fundamental description of the consciousness-body relationship, the reality of movement as it is lived by any human being, is significant for dance.

If dance creates and sustains an illusion of force, that illusion is founded upon the nature of dance as it is created and presented. The question is, How is dance created and presented? If the dancer exists her body in movement as a form-in-the-making, that form-in-the-making is the dance, the foundation of the appearance of the illusion. The dancer does not exist apart from the form which she is creating and presenting: the illusion of force is a singular phenomenon. Futher, that form-in-the-making is spatially unified and temporally continuous: the illusion of force which it creates is an indivisible, cohesive whole. The description of the lived experience of body movement as a form-in-the-making thus immediately confronts us with the relationship between the dancer creating the form, and the dance, the form-in-the-making. Moreover, because it focuses upon that relationship, the description of the lived reality of movement leads ultimately to a description of the human body as symbol within the global phenomenon of the illusion. In sustaining an illusion of force, the dancer transcends the material reality of her body: she becomes the source of the illusion, a symbol within the total phenomenon of the dance. If the dancer exists her body in movement as a form-in-the-making, it must

become clear how, within that form, the dancer creates and
sustains an illusion of force.

In pursuing an explication of the foundation and inherent
structures of the illusion which dance creates, we have thus
moved from a description of the body as mere physical phenomenon, to a description of the lived experience of body movement,
a consciousness-body relationship, wherein the moving body is
experienced as a form-in-the-making. Dance, although something more than the phenomenon of body movement, is nothing
less than the phenomenon of body movement. Hence, within
the context of dance, we are immediately directed to a description of the dancer as the moving center of a moving form: What
is the relationship between the dancer and the form, and how is
the form created as a spatial-temporal totality?

It is clear that on the pre-reflective level, the dancer and the
dance are one. The dancer is not conscious of the form-in-the-
making, the dance, as an object, and neither is she explicitly
aware of herself as she creates the form. Insofar as she is
implicitly aware of herself and the form which she is creating,
the dancer is not aware of herself as existing totally at any one
point in space or at any single moment in time: she is continually surpassing herself to a space beyond and a time future by
her very movement. Similarly, the form-in-the-making, the form
which she is creating, does not exist totally at any one point in
space or at any single instant in time: it, likewise, is continually
moving toward a spatial-temporal future. Both the dancer and
the dance exist in an *ekstatic* relationship to themselves; they are
both their own past, present, and future, spatially and temporally, in the mode of not being any one of these at any one
moment or point; they are both always in flight, always both
ahead of and behind themselves. The term *ekstatic* describes the
inevitable distance separating the dancer and the dance from
being the totality which they are, fully and wholly, at any one
moment or point. Yet, because they exist *ekstatically*, they are

spatially unified and temporally continuous: there are no moments or points which divide their spatial-temporal presence. Furthermore, and most significantly, their spatial unity and temporal continuity are one and the same. Because the dancer is pre-reflectively engaged in the creation of the dance, because she is not reflecting upon it as something apart from herself, her spatiality and temporality do not exist apart from the dance, and neither do the spatiality and temporality of the dance exist apart from her. There is but one spatiality and one temporality, and each is founded upon the dancer's lived experience of the dance. So long as the dancer exists her body in movement as a form-in-the-making, that form-in-the-making spatializes and temporalizes itself, such that the illusion which it creates and sustains is spatially and temporally all of a piece.

The spatial unity and temporal continuity of the form-in-the-making may be described further in terms of its diasporatic nature. It exists as a trajectory exists, not at any single instant or point, but in the whole of the phenomenon which the moving force creates. It is therefore both a dispersed unity and a coherent multiplicity: it is a spatial-temporal totality, a unified and continuous creation, which exists across a multiplicity of instants and points; at the same time, it is precisely the uniqueness of the inter-relationship of those instants and points which makes it uniquely meaningful. So long as the dancer is one with the dance, what is created and presented is a complete and unified phenomenon, an illusion of force, whose meaning suffuses the whole and derives from the uniqueness of that whole.

Yet, although the created and presented phenomenon may be dance, an audience itself can shatter the illusion of force. If the audience constitutes the dancer as an object, as a physically moving entity, apart from the dance, what it sees is an actual body exerting itself in a variety of ways: a vigorous jump, a delicate balance on one leg, and so on. The audience is thus reflecting upon the phenomenon being presented; it is not pre-reflectively engaged in the experience of that phenomenon. In the immediate encounter with dance, what appears is what is being created: an illusion, a sheer appearance of force.

The dancer sustains the primary illusion so long as she never separates herself from the spatial unity and temporal continuity of the form. It is only as the dancer reflects upon herself apart from the dance that she is no longer one with it, and in consequence, destroys the illusion. It is evident in performance when a dancer becomes explicitly aware of herself. As soon as she becomes self-conscious, the audience is aware of a separation of the dancer from the dance. What appears, then, is not a single phenomenon, an illusion of force, but a physical body and movement which emanates from that body. The body and the movement appear as separate and distinct phenomena because the dancer is no longer pre-reflectively aware of her body in movement as a form-in-the-making. She may exist apart from the form, for example, because she is moving through it as a pre-formed object instead of allowing the form to move through her as she creates it; because she is reflecting upon where she is now and where she must move to; or because, being nervous about her technical proficiency to execute a given movement, she is reflecting upon her ability to maintain balance. Whatever the reason might be, the separation is obvious when it occurs: it shatters what was an illusion and a totality. But as far as is evident, no one has been concerned with the question, What is a dancer conscious of while dancing? In what way must consciousness exist its body in movement for movement to become dance and be sustained as dance?

It is immediately apparent that the dancer who is one with the dance, and who thereby creates and sustains an illusion of force, is pre-reflectively aware of her body in movement as a form-in-the-making. She is not reflecting upon what her body is doing, nor what she is doing with her body, but exists it at each moment and point pre-reflectively; she never qualifies herself as being wholly at any given moment or point, for she is always both ahead of and behind herself. It is this very flight, this continual surpassing or perpetual creation, which allows the dancer to create and apprehend the dance as a totality and as an illusion of force.

It is on a reflective level that the dancer construes her body in movement as an object. In establishing the form-in-the-making as an objective form, the dancer destroys the internal spatial and temporal structure of the form, such that neither the form nor the dancer are capable of being a spatial-temporal totality: the spatial-temporal dimensions of the form and the body are dispersed into an externally related sequence of discrete moments in time and isolated points in space. The form and the body no longer exist *ekstatically*. In consequence, the dance is presented not as having an *ekstatic* structure, by virtue of the dancer being one with the dance, but as an object outside or separate from the dancer, an object incapable of spatializing or temporalizing itself. What appears to the audience, then, is a succession of points and moments which can be made continuous only by a consciousness which is external to them. But it is questionable whether a dance presented as an object distinct from the dancer is, or even can be, endowed by the audience with an internally related spatial-temporal structure.

On both the pre-reflective and reflective levels of consciousness, the original existential spatial-temporal definitions of the human body, its physical spatial unity and temporal continuity, are retained as the foundation of the more complex spatial-temporal definitions of the human body in movement, where the consciousness-body relationship is described. Thus, even as the dancer reflects upon her body as an object, that physical body is nevertheless spatially unified and temporally continuous. What is not spatially unified and temporally continuous at that reflective level is the movement of the body. When the form-in-the-making is pushed outside consciousness to exist as an object, the spatial-temporal aspects of the form lose their internal unification and continuity, and the illusion of force is shattered:

movement becomes actual effort, actual exertion, actual force, taking place in an objective space-time. It is only on the pre-reflective level, when consciousness exists its body in movement as a form-in-the-making, that the movement is spatially unified and temporally continuous. And only when the movement is spatially unified and temporally continuous, when the dancer creating the form and the form-in-the-making exist diasporatically within the same *ekstatic* structure, does the form-in-the-making create and sustain a sheer appearance of force.

If virtual force is the descriptive analogue of dance, if it describes what is immediately created and presented, and if dance is created and presented as a form-in-the-making, then virtual force is a force which temporalizes and spatializes itself within the phenomenal field. The foregoing descriptions of the relationship between the dancer and the dance, and of the spatial-temporal aspects of that relationship, make clear that the form-in-the-making, while founded upon the lived experience of movement in everyday life, is a form which creates an illusion of force. It exists within a particular, aesthetic context, which is different from either the practical or the affective context of everyday life: it creates and sustains *a sheer appearance of force.* Virtual force is thereby the essence of all dance, but is uniquely qualified by its very spatialization and temporalization in each particular dance. If it were not so, all dances would be the same: if all dances were nothing more than an undifferentiated virtual force, there would be nothing unique about any one of them. On the contrary, each dance *is* different and its singular difference relates in part to the highly individualized manner in which virtual force is temporalized and spatialized, in which virtual force is projected as a unique form-in-the-making. Yet although virtual force is the condition of all dance, it is not a specifiable thing in any dance: dance appears not as a part by part · revelation of force, but as a perpetual revelation of force which, by creating its own unique time and space, sustains an illusion of force. The form-in-the-making describes this perpetual creation, this movement of form toward its own completion. Virtual force, then, is an illusion of force which spatializes and temporalizes itself; it takes place neither in the space and time of everyday life nor outside these dimensions altogether. A comparison with the space and time of everyday life will, in fact, point up the distinction more clearly.

It will be readily admitted that dance can be considered an event taking place in time and in space, which continue to exist as objective structures both before the beginning and after the completion of the dance. It would therefore be quite logical to assume that time and space are infinite containers filled with events taking place in the world. But how, one may ask, would these events or momentary events within the larger events be inter-connected? And what would constitute the basis for their relationship to one another? What, in other words, makes the dance a totality if it is merely a succession of externally related "events" or movements? To answer that the feeling quality, motif, or idea, of a dance unites the series of spatial-temporal moments suggests that these can themselves be temporally and spatially segmented into a series of befores and afters, for how can feeling quality, motif, or idea be spatially unified and temporally continuous if they take place as events in time and in space? To describe feeling quality in terms of a series of longer, shorter, faster, or slower intervals, for example, or as so many changes of direction or full turns, is to describe analytically a relationship one sees between feeling quality and actual movement and not feeling quality and dance. Dance is a totality which, though dispersed, remains a unity. To describe feeling quality in such a way is also to reduce the dance to a set of counters, each of which represents a particular and absolute meaning, such that the feeling quality is no more than the sum of these individual meanings.

In order to discover the spatial unity and temporal continuity of dance, it is necessary to look at the total phenomenal presence of dance and see what is immediately there. Since a dance is a complete and unified form, the space and time of the dance are also a totality, whose elements can be viewed separately, but can never exist in isolation one from another. Past, present, and future constitute an inviolable synthesis, both spatially and temporally. Past, present, and future exist within the total phenomenon of the dance itself. There is not a succession of externally related movements, for from the beginning what will occur in the future is contained within what occurred in the past, and what occurred in the past is retained within that which occurs in the future.

The time and space of the dance may, in fact, be further clarified in relation to their internal organization within the dance. They are different from either the objective or lived experience of time and space in everyday life: each particular organization of past-present-future within the dance forms a specific spatiality and temporality which particularizes the illusion of force. Because any dance presents a highly differentiated organization, each dance is an entirely original work; it is thoroughly unique in the way in which it unfolds across its own spatial-temporal dimensions. The very first movement of a dance contains within itself its own singular realm of possibilities; it presents a germinal quality which, even in embryonic form, contains the potentialities of its spatial-temporal future. The dance, then, projects itself as a unique spatial-temporal totality even across its unfinished form, as it is composed and as it is presented.

Finally, the time and space of each dance are unique in that, in terms of the very first movement, the dance has no past, and in terms of the very last movement, it has no future. It is this very lack which explicitly differentiates the time and space of the dance from the time and space of everyday life. A dance cuts into everyday time and space. Its past and future come into being only at the moment the dance is present in the beginning movement; and its future is a possibility only until the moment the dance is no longer present. Hence, apart from its creation and presentation, the dance has no spatial-temporal existence. It is apparent, then, that the temporality and spatiality of the dance, while founded upon the lived experience of time and space in everyday life, are structures within the total structure of the illusion which dance creates. They are integral parts of the total creation. Thus, on the primary ontological level, space and time are neither secondary illusions, nor do they externally support virtual force; rather, they are intrinsic dimensions of it. On the pre-reflective level, virtual force is inherently spatialized and temporalized by the dancer as she creates the form. On the reflective level, virtual force is made to be spatially unified and temporally continuous by a consciousness which, while contemplating the form-in-the-making from the outside, attempts to endow it with *ekstatic* dimensions. Virtual force therefore exists either as a highly individualized spatial-temporal totality, or an attempt is made to apprehend it as such; it is either internally related by a pre-reflective consciousness or externally related by a reflective consciousness. But the question arises, as suggested earlier, whether virtual force can be either internally or externally unified and either internally or externally continuous. Is there an option? To answer this question, we must consider how virtual force emanates from an actual human body, how the body becomes a symbol within the total phenomenon of the illusion.

If the body transforms its physical reality and becomes, as Mrs. Langer states, ". . . a created personality, a dance element which figures simply as a psychical, human or superhuman Being," [3] and if this Being is a center of force, as Mrs. Langer continues, then neither the movement, the force which it projects, nor the body, the center of force, can be created or presented as a discrete spatial series or temporal sequence. If the primary illusion is to be sustained, both must be spatially unified and temporally continuous: in the world of illusion, there can be no

3. Langer, *Feeling and Form*, p. 181.

dimensions, or rather, the dimensions of time and space can themselves have no objective dimensional values. If everything is pure appearance, there can be no division into discrete moments and isolated points; these would have to be non-existent. In looking at dance, we see that this is so, but it is not yet clear how this distillation of reality is effected. How does the body in dance become, in effect, a virtual body so that as it moves, it creates and is seen as creating a continuous and unified form? If, as Mrs. Langer has affirmed, the dancer herself is a symbol within the total form of the dance, and if to be a symbol is to have a common logical form in terms of the thing symbolized, then the dancer as symbol and as actual consciousness-body must be logically related.

On the purely physical level, the body as symbol is logically related to the actual human body: the way in which the body can move does not change. It is still governed by the laws of motion, by its anatomical structure, and the like. There is thus on the purely physical level an absolute congruity of form. However, as pure appearance, as symbol, the body in movement is not intuited within the natural dimensions of the body—as a torso with head, arms, and legs, as flexing and extending, as "giving in" to gravity, etc. If the body is the source of the illusion, then its physical dimensions cannot be measured, since such measurements would break the body into spatial-temporal parts and assessment of spatial-temporal values could be made upon it. Hence, the body as symbol is related to the dancer's pre-reflective awareness of her body. The dancer is not conscious of her leg and how long she must keep her leg extended in the air, nor of her arm and how far she must abduct her arm. She cannot reflect upon her body in movement as an object and make it exist apart from the form she is creating, without immediately breaking the spatial unity and temporal continuity of the dance into discrete points and instants. Similarly, the audience is not aware of how long a dancer's leg is extended, or to what extent her arm is abducted. If the audience reflects upon the dance as it is being presented, it destroys the illusion of force by dividing it into discrete moments and points and ascribing values which are non-existent within the world of illusion.

It is therefore evident that the common logical form between dancer as symbol and as actual consciousness-body can go deeper than the absolute congruity of physical forms. The lived experience of the body, the pre-reflective awareness of the body in everyday life, is readily apparent. Insofar as we are enmeshed in the affective and practical conditions of living, we do not make an object of our body, reflect upon it as something separate from ourselves. In like manner, the movement of our body is not made to be an object either, unless perhaps we are learning some new skill and focus attention upon the manner in which we are moving. A pre-reflective awareness of the body and the body in movement exists in everyday life. It is phenomenologically evident that someone in grief, for example, is implicitly aware of his body as feeling grief; the body is part of the lived experience, not something distinct from it. Similarly, someone in anger is implicitly aware of his fist plummeting down onto a table; he does not reflect upon being angry and then decide to make a fist and bang it on the table. The fist and the bang are spontaneous and apparent aspects of the feeling. If the anger is reflected upon first, then the body and the body movement are made to be objects. In an affective context of everyday life, a pre-reflective awareness of the body and the body in movement is supported *by actual feeling*. In dance, a pre-reflective awareness of the body and the body in movement is supported *by the form* of a feeling.

Within the lived experience of movement it is clearly the *ekstatic* structure of consciousness-body which is the fundamental point of congruence between the dancer as symbol and as actual consciousness-body. The dance is a symbol of a form of human feelings and is presented by a symbol of the human who feels those feelings in everyday life. The human who feels those feelings as lived experiences in everyday life is pre-reflectively aware of himself through his affective consciousness-body; that is, not as reflectively clenching his fists in anger, not as reflectively opening his arms in a gesture of fond greeting, but as implicitly aware of himself in these movements as he moves. As such, they are segmented neither into discrete spatial points nor discrete temporal moments, but exist as a totality. In an affective context of everyday life, consciousness exists its body in movement as a form-in-the-making which is a *form of feeling*, and a spatial unity and temporal continuity exist because at this pre-reflective level, consciousness exists in an *ekstatic* relationship to itself. In dance, consciousness exists its body in movement as a form-in-the-making which is a *sheer form*, and a spatial unity and temporal continuity exist because at this pre-reflective level, consciousness-body is likewise implicitly aware of its *ekstatic* structure.

Beyond this, we can look at the phenomenon of the lived experience of movement itself to find a further congruity between the dancer as symbol and as actual consciousness-body. Whether the lived experience is the plummeting of a fist upon the table, or the creation of a dance, the lived experience exists diasporatically: while there are no divisions within the totality of the movement as it is lived, it is the inter-relationship of the unique and particular units within the total kinetic experience which gives it its unique meaning. Because both phenomena, by virtue of their *ekstatic* structure, are dispersed yet cohesive phenomena; because both, while existing across a multiplicity of instants and points, exist nevertheless as a unique totality and a totality which is uniquely meaningful, they are logically related: it is of the nature of each to be a unified multiplicity and a multiple unity.

The symbolic form of dance exists within the total phenomenon of the illusion of force which each dance creates. But the dancer as symbol exists also within the global phenomenon of the illusion: in her lived experience of a dance, the dancer is one with the symbolic form. It is not a question of two symbols being present because the dancer does not exist apart from the dance—any more than the person who is angry exists apart from the plummeting of his fist upon the table. Hence, to speak of the dancer as symbol is actually to speak of the dancer as a center of force. Insofar as she exists her body in movement as a *sheer* form-in-the-making, she is the source of the illusion of force which that form creates.

It is clear, then, that the foundational *ekstatic* structure which is the basis for the spatial unity and temporal continuity of the dance is also the basis for the dancer's being a symbol within the total phenomenon of the dance. The dancer and the dance cannot be specified at any one point in space or at any single instant in time because of their singular *ekstatic* structure; both necessarily exist outside any such concrete spatial and temporal values. The difference between the spatial-temporal aspects of actual force and virtual force is rooted in the fact that in the latter, there is no possibility of dividing space or time into points or moments, for no such actual dimensional values appear within the world of illusion, without thereby destroying the illusion. Once the dancer ceases to exist her body in movement as a form-in-the-making, and instead apprehends it as an object, the illusion dies, and the audience cannot endow a serialized presented form with an *ekstatic* structure without perceiving what is there to be something which is not there. If it were possible for the audience to endow the form with an *ekstatic* structure, then the audience, in effect, would be the creator of dance.

The sheer form-in-the-making which is dance exists within the totally differentiated modality of the illusion. Its spatiality and temporality are neither secondary illusions nor external supportive devices; rather, they are intrinsic structures which allow the primary illusion to be sustained. Space and time are created and uniquely created with each dance: as the form-in-the-making perpetually reveals itself as an illusion of force, it reveals itself as a highly individualized illusion.

CHAPTER IV

THE PLASTIC COMPONENTS

OF VIRTUAL FORCE

Each dance presents an illusion of force which is always present yet never totally present, any more than the dance is totally present at any one moment or point. This is because the actual components of force are transformed: they are no longer isolable and distinct factors of actual movement, but interrelated qualities of virtual force. They are qualities rather than actual components because the form in which they exist is a totally differentiated form, one which is symbolically expressive. Furthermore, the very plasticity of the components, the very fact that they can be freely created and developed according to the demands of the form, makes the symbolically expressive form possible. If these components could not be freely developed apart from any actual affective or situational context, they could not be anything but actual components of actual movement;

they could not be the substance of a symbolic form and appear as qualities of virtual force.

There are several points to be noted in preface to a description of these components. Since their plasticity has to do with their potential appearance in a symbolic form, they will be described as *qualities*. We will, in other words, look at these components of force as plastic, as they potentially exist for dance rather than as they actually exist in a specific movement in everyday life. It is important to emphasize, however, that these qualities exist only insofar as virtual force exists, only insofar as dance is created, in the same way that the temporal and spatial structures of virtual force exist only insofar as dance is created. The qualities, as such, are neither additive nor discrete: one quality is not appended to another quality and then another quality to make up the illusion of force, and neither does any quality engender a significance in and of itself. It is not a question of putting specifically chosen qualities together and arranging them in a certain way, nor is it a question of each quality or all of the qualities combined, having a denotative or connotative significance in and of itself. Phenomenologically, no quality exists apart from the unique *Gestalt* which any particular movement presents, and neither the quality nor the particular movement has significance apart from the total dance.

If we look at the phenomenon of movement, at its pure appearance untied to any actual affective or practical condition, movement appears as a *revelation of force;* it appears in and of itself as power or energy. All qualities of movement are therefore describable in relation to the global phenomenon of force: each quality describes a particular and apparent structure of movement as a revelation of force.

Tensional, linear, areal, and projectional qualities [1] are present

1. These terms describe the qualitative structures of the total illusion of force. As far as is known, they have never before been used. They emanate from the author's own experience of movement as a revelation of force.

in movement as a revelation of force. Movement as a revelation of force synthesizes these qualities and causes them to be mutually influential: the particular definition of one quality will affect the particular definition of the other qualities. For example, the linear quality of any movement does not exist apart from the tension required to project the line, the area displaced in creating the line, nor the manner in which the line is projected. All qualities of movement are internally bound to one another in and through movement, in and through force which is the global structure of the presented phenomenon.

Tensional quality very often refers to the amount of effort exerted by the body through muscular contraction. Although tension may refer to a measurable quantity, it is only as quality that tension can function in dance. What appears as tensional quality in any revelation of force is not a relatively strong or a relatively weak contraction, but the absolute tensional quality of a particular revelation of force. For example, in going from an upright position into a "hinge" position to the floor—flexing the knees so that the body tilts diagonally backwards until the shoulders touch the floor—the dancer exerts a great amount of force; yet, the apparent force of the movement is not necessarily great. The body may appear to "sink," the movement may appear almost effortless. Thus, we have a clear example of the distinct difference between a component of actual force, and a quality of virtual force. Any quality of virtual force does not exist until the symbolic form of dance is created; and when the symbolic form is created, the quality is not something which may be measured, compared, or judged in any way in and of itself. It may only be described as it appears in the total form, and its existence in the total form is nothing more than its immediate appearance.

In reference to muscular contraction, tension is described as an actual component of actual force: a strong, moderate, or weak contraction is adjudged the source of power for the movement. Such a description of tension is, in fact, an explanation of its causal sequence and not a description of its apparent manifestations. In looking at movement, we see tensional quality projected, and in our immediate intuition, we are oblivious of the degree of contraction involved. It is therefore evident that it is through reflection that tension is constituted as an actual component of actual movement; only in reflecting upon movement can we look at tension as an isolable particular which has significance in and of itself: we can focus upon it as a distinct thing and attempt a determination of its value.

As a quality of force, tension is visually apparent, yet from the dancer's point of view it is kinesthetically apparent. This seeming complexity of tensional quality is not so puzzling, however, if one considers that *amount of force refers not to a contained, static amount held by the body, but to the manifest dynamic of the projection itself.* Tensional quality exists only as it is projected in and through movement, and any particular movement will dissipate a particular tensional quality. The significant point is that phenomenologically, tensional quality is there, immediately apparent in the movement, whether kinesthetically or visually: it is the intensity or magnitude of the specific force being projected, its *qualitative* strength, vigor, or potency. But it is even more than this: the projected tensional quality is the very force itself which is being revealed, and as such, it characterizes the force as being this particular force and none other. It is clear, then, that although the projected tensional quality certainly derives from the tensional state of the body, it is only as the tensional state reveals force that one can speak of the tensional quality of movement. And when the tensional quality is revealed, it is the very pith of the movement itself, the very particular force being projected.

Movement as a revelation of force also presents a linear quality which describes both the linear design of the body as it moves and the linear pattern created by the body as it moves. The body's linear design is the line the body segments make singly or in combination, and the line which the body presents as a whole. It may be curved, twisted, angular, diagonal, vertical, etc., or any combination of such linear segments. The linear design is a directional line, the directional attitude the body projects as it moves. It is thus inclusive of those parts which are "held" as well as of those which are moving. For example, the legs and torso may be held in a vertical position while the arms move sequentially up and down. The linear design of the body is the total directional configuration of the moving force: the "constant" verticality, and the "variable" curvilinearity.

The linear pattern which the moving body describes is likewise a directional line, for movement as a revelation of force is projected along linear paths. The linear pattern is the result of the direction in which the body as a moving force projects itself: diagonally, in a zig-zag manner, circularly, etc. A more complete discussion of linear quality will be presented in Chapter IX where the total spatialization of force in dance will be described. It suffices to note here that linear quality is apparent in the directional design and pattern of body movement as a revelation of force.

One aspect of linear quality may be mentioned here, however, which is neither wholly design nor pattern, and this aspect is focus. Focus creates a non-existent line from the eyes (or the body) to their directional point of contact. Focus is a directional aspect of movement, but a peculiar one in that no moving force is presented as establishing the direction. Focus might be described as an intended but undrawn line which either by contrast or emphasis influences the total spatiality created by any movement. For example, if a dancer were moving in a straight line forward, but kept the eyes focused upon the ground, a directional line downward would be created in addition to the vertical design of the body and the straight forward linear pattern of the movement. Similarly, if the eyes focused straight ahead, the straight forward linear pattern of the movement would be emphasized.

A third quality of movement as a revelation of force concerns the range or shape of the force, and like linear quality, it has two distinct aspects: areal design and areal pattern.[2] Areal quality is present in the shape of the body, its areal design, and in the shape of the created dance space, areal pattern. The areal design of the body may be anywhere from contractive to expansive depending upon the amplitude of the body as a center of force. If the created shape of the body is small and compact, for example, the areal design of the body as a center of force appears contractive. Similarly, the areal pattern of the movement may be anywhere from intensive to extensive, contained or diffused, depending upon the amplitude of the force as it is projected.

Dance occurs on a stage area, but this area is not the created space of the dance. A dance creates its own space within or beyond the boundaries of the stage area. This created space is, in part, qualitatively defined by the areal pattern. The total stage area may become the created space of a dance if movement is projected across the entire stage area. But it is also apparent that a dance may nullify the actual boundaries or limitations which the actual stage area poses because it creates its own space. A dance may appear as being more extensive than the total stage area, for example, through an extensive areal pattern, a diagonal linear pattern, and through the phenomenon of focus. A complete explication of the created space of dance will be found in a later chapter.

The terms used to define the gamut of a particular quality must not be considered as postulating an either-or relationship; that is, if one is not contractive, he is expansive, if the projected force is not vigorous, it is flaccid, if the pattern is not intensive, it is extensive, and so on. There is simply a lack of names by which all of the innumerable intermediary qualities may be known.

2. "Area" and "areal" as used in the text of this book are not metric functions. They do not designate a two-dimensional measurement in space or of space. Rather, they designate the three-dimensional spatial shape of the body and body movement. There is no word which denotes these ever-changing shapes; hence, the choice of a word which at least connotes a fluid, moldable mass and expanse.

This is to say that they are actually presented, but because a comprehensive movement vocabulary is lacking, they are inexpressible. Because the vocabulary is limited, too, one often has recourse to quantitative terms, comparisons of amount such as more contracted, moderate tension, smaller range, etc. But the quantitative pitfall may be avoided to a degree by relating a qualitative aspect of force to its larger phenomenal structure, rather than to other instances of the same quality. Thus, one would look at any given movement of a dance not as exhibiting a stronger tensional quality than another movement, but rather, as revealing a tensional quality which logically or illogically manifests itself at a specific point in the context of the total dance, which logically or illogically is related to the development of the form-in-the-making, and so to the particular revelation of force. For example, if in the context of a dance, the line of the arm and hand were broken at the wrist, the hand making a ninety degree angle with the arm, and if such a line obtruded, appearing as an anomaly within the context of the total dance, the linear quality of the particular movement might be described as being "illogical." We may note in conjunction with this example that when any quality is "illogical" in the context of the total dance, the illusion of force which the dance creates is destroyed, for the quality is really no longer a quality of virtual force, but an actual component of movement: the single and flagrant line of the arm and hand which disturbs the coherency and flow of the moving form by appearing as a thing in and of itself apart from the dance.

A second comment may be made concerning the limited vocabulary of movement. The terms used in speaking of movement are static, positional terms: contractive, vertical, etc. Any attempt to illustrate a quality seems to stop the body so that the illustration seems more a description of position than of movement. It would, of course, be possible to describe a movement using anatomical and kinesiological terms of reference, but such descriptions have been deliberately omitted as being so complex as to overshadow the purpose of the description. In addition, they would not coincide with the phenomenological nature of this descriptive study: they would not describe movement as it appears. The terms which are and have been used must be considered dynamic. For example, to speak of the body's linear design as being vertical means that the body is continuing to exert the verticality of its projected force as it moves. Thus, while parts of the body may be "held" in a certain position, they are held dynamically. Similarly, to say that the areal quality of a dance is contractive means that the areal design of the body as a center of force is predominantly compact, tight, or close; it does not mean that the body never expands beyond an original contractive shape.

The final quality of movement as a revelation of force is projectional quality, the manner in which force is projected. Very generally, three different qualities are possible: abrupt, sustained, and ballistic. Again it may be noted that these classifications are not rigid. Because any particular designation is inclusive of infinite degrees of shading, there are innumerable intermediary qualities which separate an abrupt movement from a sustained movement, a sustained movement from a ballistic movement, etc. Furthermore, a given projectional quality may present any combination of the three basic ones. However, to describe generally the manner in which force may be projected, it is apparent that the body may project force all at once and move abruptly; it may attenuate the projection and move in a sustained manner; or it may project force initially, allow forces such as gravity, momentum, and inertia to influence it, and hence move in a ballistic manner. The force the body is projecting is a specific tensional quality. As such, it is sometimes wrongfully assumed that an abrupt movement is always vigorous and explosive, and that a sustained movement is always weak and delicate. On the contrary, given any tensional quality which represents a specific potency of force to be projected, that projection may be in any manner desired. There are, as indicated previously, no predetermined or absolute significances within the total dance; the form-in-the-making is an interrelationship of qualities which have no set meaning in and of themselves, but which may be developed freely according to the demands of the form.

Projectional quality, as is evident, has something to do with the spatial-temporal structure of movement, and so with the time and space of the dance; the manner in which force is projected creates a specific temporality in reference to any given movement, and it also creates a particular spatialization of force. For example, an abrupt movement of the head to the side creates a temporality and spatiality distinct from the same movement projected in a sustained manner. This highly significant aspect of projectional quality will be fully discussed in Chapters VII, VIII, and IX, where the created time and space of the dance will be described in detail.

All the qualities which compose virtual force have been only briefly recounted here. Their complete elaboration must await further development; they must be described from a compositional as well as a "finished dance" point of view. Thus far, the emphasis has been on dance as it is presented in order to find out what is there, what dance is in the fullest possible sense: it is the creation of an illusion of force which is spatially unified and temporally continuous; the illusion is created and sustained by a form-in-the-making which is itself spatially unified and temporally continuous; the form-in-the-making is created and presented through movement which appears as a revelation of force; and finally, the actual components of force which underlie the illusion of force are plastic, and as such, are transformed into qualities of movement as a revelation of force.

We have begun with the thing itself and will work "backwards" from this point. Such an approach has been taken because any conception of dance must be founded upon the lived experience of dance itself. Dance cannot be deduced from theoretical speculation about movement, from principles of composition, or whatever; it can only be described as the thing which it is. We must now look further at the phenomenon of dance in order to describe the nature of a form which creates and sustains an illusion of force; specifically, how the actual components of force become plastic so that a symbolic form may be created.

CHAPTER V

ABSTRACTION

Abstraction is inherent in the creation of a symbolic form. Through abstraction the symbolic form achieves a significance in and of itself; its meaning or import is intrinsic to it. There are two abstractions apparent in the creation of the symbolic form of dance. The first has to do with the forms of actual human feeling which are abstracted from their everyday context in order to be created and presented symbolically, and the second has to do with movement which is abstracted from its everyday expressive context to become the expressive medium of dance. Through abstraction the forms of human feeling exist in a new context which is symbolic, and movement exists in a new context which is symbolically expressive rather than symptomatically or referentially so. The two abstractions relate to the form and the medium of dance, but both aim toward the realization of a single symbolic form because they occur simultaneously: the form never exists apart from the movement and the movement never exists apart from the form. We may look at the form and movement separately only because each is an analyzable structure within the total dance, but it must be emphasized that neither exists separately within the total dance. What must be described fully in reference to each abstraction is not only what is abstracted, but the consequence of the abstraction in relation to the total symbolic form.

If the form of actual human feeling is abstracted from everyday life, the nature of that form must first be clarified. We must distinguish the form of a human feeling from the content of a human feeling. The content of a human feeling in everyday life may be described as an affective response or an affective consciousness occurring in-the-midst-of-the-world. It is a particular feeling and none other, here and now. The meaning of a human feeling in everyday life is usually taken to be in the content, in the pangs of the affected consciousness. For example, the meaning of fear is in the feeling of being fearful, and not in the form of the fear. The content is what gives the feeling a contextual significance in everyday life.

The form of a human feeling in everyday life may be described as the pattern of development of the feeling: the way in which it endures—its suspensions and lulls, its quicknesses and slownesses—and the way in which it fluctuates and is marked by changes in intensity—its strong peaks and weak ebbs. A form of actual human feeling has an apparent structure: the form pulsates in a particular way. Furthermore, there is a continuum of form in everyday life because there is a continuum of feeling. A specific form within the continuum is not pre-determined in the sense of its being a lived experience; a form of anger, for example, is not a rigidly set pattern which develops in a prescribed fashion, nor some pre-existing form into which the person fits his feeling of anger. Any number of forms may clothe

the same content in everyday life which is to say that the same feeling may achieve a variety of forms. Finally, the form of a particular feeling in everyday life never exists as a complete form except diasporatically or in memory, for it never exists fully, all at once.

If the form of human feeling is abstracted from everyday life, if the mere pattern of human feeling is considered apart from the everyday continuum and apart from specific contents, it is a *sheer dynamic form*, a form which unfolds in a certain way, which moves from its incipient stages to a fullness and a denouement. As soon as the form is abstracted it becomes a potential symbol, for it is logically congruent with forms of actual feeling. The rises and falls, concentrations and diffusions, attenuations and eruptions exist in their own right and become symbolic of the form of actual human feeling. To abstract the form of human feeling, then, is to abstract the sheer dynamic patterns of sentience from everyday life in order to render them symbolically.

It is clear that the form of dance is therefore an abstracted form in two senses: it is abstracted from the continuum of form in everyday life to exist as a complete form in and of itself—it needs no prologue or epilogue, no past or future referents to make it logical or complete—and secondly, it is abstracted from actual content so that it is divorced from any actual and specific feeling. We look at the form of dance and see it not as holding a specific content but as being significant in and of itself, not as being an actual expression of joy, for example, but as being a symbol of a form of joyfulness.

In respect to the second way in which the form of dance is abstracted, one may ask why the significance of the form is not merely a new content. If the form no longer clothes a specific affective response of consciousness, but exists in and of itself, it is no longer the means by which an actual affective meaning exists, but a concrete symbol of a form of that affective meaning.

It is presumably for this reason that Mrs. Langer speaks of the *import* of an abstracted form rather than its content or meaning, for "import" commonly implies a kind of meaning which suffuses a whole and is inseparable from that whole. The question, What is abstracted? must therefore lead to a further understanding of how form without content becomes, in effect, form reflecting import. What we must look for is a description of the consequence of the abstracted form of dance.

The term "import," as suggested above, does not refer to a specific thing: neither to a thing which exists at any moment or point in the dance, nor to a thing which exists separately from the form. Import is reflected by the form and is therefore related to the vital, qualitative pattern of the form. Import is dynamic: the form does not hold import but reflects it as the form itself is presented. Because the form is a form-in-the-making, a form which moves and changes, its import, too, is vital and moving. To describe import, then, is to recognize once more the diasporatic nature of the form: the import is not a particular isolable in the form, it is not something which is recognized independently from the form, and it is not deduced from the form; it is immediately reflected by it.

If we look at a specific dance, Martha Graham's *Lamentation*, for example, the import can neither be stated in so many words nor pointed to as residing at any particular moment or place in the dance. It moves through the dance and is reflected by the total work. Even if one were to describe the import of *Lamentation* as "an overwhelming sense of grief," this verbal translation of the dance is in no way equivalent to the import of the dance itself. It is merely an attempt to specify the import verbally, to translate from one symbolic system, dance, into another, language; and the expressions in the two symbolic systems are in no way synonymous, but two different expressions. Verbal designations are furthermore not equivalent to the import because they cannot capture the particular import of a particular dance: several dances may be "sad," so that the same verbal designation can in no way capture the uniqueness of the particular import of a particular dance.[1]

Import may not be pointed to in the dance because it follows the diasporatic nature of the abstracted form. Nor may import be reduced atomistically to a set of counters which have specific meanings: the stamping of a foot or a lunge in the context of a dance has no absolute significance in and of itself. The import is a function of the dance as a whole, and the very fact that the form-in-the-making is a moving form precludes the possibility of grasping the dance in its wholeness, all at once. Just as the form-in-the-making is neither a thing of distinct temporal moment nor of distinct spatial point, so the import of the form-in-the-making is not a temporally or spatially discrete entity. It cannot be demonstrated in, nor reduced to, a single movement phrase. It suffuses a whole, but a whole which never exists totally in a given moment. The wholeness exists either as a present in the context of a cumulative past and an anticipated future, or as a cumulative whole in memory. Hence, the import at any moment or point in a dance exists only in the internal spatial-temporal relationship of past-present-future; and the import of the dance as a whole is in the retention of what the diasporatically presented whole reflects.

But what is reflected? What is the import of a dance? The import is what the dance is in and of itself. In order to talk about what the dance is in and of itself, one must name specific feelings, not as verbal equivalents nor as approximate verbal designations of the import, but as linguistic symbols of the *pure phenomena* of feelings. The import of a dance is the *pure*

---

1. Reference may be made to Croce's theory: ". . . expression is a species which cannot function in its turn as a genus." Croce speaks of the impossibility of translations ". . . insofar as they pretend to effect the re-moulding of one expression into another . . . every translation either diminishes and spoils, or it creates a new expression. . . ." (*Aesthetic*, trans. Douglas Ainslie, New York, 1960, p. 68.) Croce is speaking specifically of literary translations, but it is obvious that his remarks hold true for any translation whatsoever of a work of art.

phenomenon of joy, fear, or whatever, untied to any actual situational context, separate from any everyday life affective consciousness, symbolically presented through a sheer form of the feeling. The actual feeling is not present; only a symbol of a form of that feeling is present. Import is therefore something which exists only by virtue of the symbolic form. There is no actual and original import from which a symbolic import is abstracted.

If the import of a dance relates to a feeling which the symbolic form reflects, then clearly, the audience can only intuit the import of a dance through its formal presentation. But the intuition of the import is concurrent with the intuition of the presented form: the symbol always combines a mutually determined concrete form and meaning of some order. When we look at a dance, we do not see the mere organized surface, the mere movement as movement, but the organized surface as it reflects import. The two things are merged in a single intuition. Because import is inherent in the dance, not something existing apart from the form of the dance, we, as audience, intuit the import with the form. We are not interpreting on a reflective level while the dance is being performed. If we were, we would be attempting to ascribe distinct meanings to distinct movements in the dance. On the contrary, our intuition of the import follows the diasporatic nature of the form. If we are wholly and unequivocally intuiting a dance, then our intuition will necessarily be spatially unified and temporally continuous in the same manner as the import and the form of the dance. We do not have to name any feeling in order to recognize the import of the dance, but have only to intuit the dance as it is being presented in order to intuit the import which it reflects. Whether or not we wish to give verbal expression to our intuition is quite another matter, for the verbal expression is a reflection upon the dance, and is not the pre-reflective, lived experience of the dance.

It may be recalled that in Chapter III it was stated that on a pre-reflective level the audience intuits the dancer's body in movement as a form-in-the-making. This pre-reflective awareness is an immediate and direct apprehension of the form-in-the-making and the import of that form. Consciousness apprehends the form-in-the-making not as a mere organized surface—in Langer's terms, an "empty form"—but as a surface reflecting import; just as the surface is not separate from its import, so the intuition of the surface is not separate from the intuition of the import. The dance is all of a piece and the audience's intuition of the dance is all of a piece.

It is clear then that the immediate lived experience of dance is an intuition of whatever feeling the form is symbolic of. It is not an experience of actual sorrow, rage, love, jealousy, or whatever. Neither is it a matter of empathy, of "going through" the movements kinesthetically. Kinesthetic responses may certainly be present, but the import of the dance does not reside in these. The import can no more exist as the sum of these kinesthetic responses than as the sum of all the movement in the dance. True, we may be literally moved by, that is, kinesthetically respond to, a dance, but to interpret this "movement" as the import is to look upon the form of the dance as an empty form. Furthermore, it is to miss the lived experience of the dance by being reflectively preoccupied with one's own internal state. The lived experience of the dance is ineffable: it has no kinesthetic equivalents any more than it has any verbal equivalents.

It is possible now to offer a specific example to illustrate the way in which the form of dance is an abstracted form, and the consequence of this abstraction in relation to both form and import. For descriptive purposes, it will be best to consider not only an overt form of a feeling, but a feeling which has common overt forms; that is, we may think of someone who is angry and immediately think of overt forms which are common to anger. Let us, then, take a common overt form of a feeling such as someone shrugging his shoulders in resignation.

As a form of resignation, the form on a reflective level may be experienced as a two-phased form: there is a rising and a falling of the shoulders. But there is also a momentary suspension at the peak of the rise, so that the rising and falling are not two evenly projected phases. The rising phase of the form is elongated, held, as the breath is held, and the falling phase punctuates the close of the form, as the breath is sharply expelled. It is interesting to note that it is impossible to execute this form as resignation unless the breath follows the form: it is impossible to exhale while raising the shoulders and still sense the feeling of the form as resignation. The specific breath control follows the bodily expression of feeling. This cursory analysis of a form of resignation, its mere pattern of development, is concerned only with the form of a feeling as it holds content in everyday life. One could systematically analyze it according to its actual components. For example, the tensional component of the rise, the linear component of the body, the projectional component, etc. This analysis will be made subsequently when we consider the way in which movement is abstracted from everyday life. What we are concerned with here is an example of a form of actual feeling which may be abstracted, which may become a *sheer* form in and of itself. When we abstract the sheer form of the feeling, *we experience the form and not the feeling,* and we furthermore experience the form as a revelation of force, a force which grows to a crescendo and ends in an abrupt denouement. As a sheer form of feeling, the form is open to elaboration. For example, the intensity may be diminished or augmented, the denouement may be sustained rather than abrupt, the suspension may be elongated, the tempo of the complete form may be quickened, etc. If this abstracted form constituted the beginning of a dance, it is clear that the import of the dance would be embodied in and reflected by the total form. The import of the dance would not necessarily be approximated verbally to "resignation," for the import would develop only as the form is elaborated. And, in fact, the import could be approximated to a feeling having nothing to do with resignation at all.

Any sheer form of feeling is compositionally a free form. It is developed according to its own logical demands. It need not follow the exact shifts in intensity, the exact durations, the exact sequence or flow in the form of the actual feeling. The sheer form is a plastic form because it is abstracted from the continuum of feeling and affective consciousness of everyday life. It is created and presented as a concrete and significant form in its own right: it is a form which is complete in and of itself.

From a consideration of how the form of dance is an abstracted form, we may now consider how movement in dance is abstracted. The form, being a concrete abstracted form created and presented in an artistic medium, is, from the very beginning, elaborated in movement; movement is the substance of the form and, in fact, is the very form itself within the context of the dance. We may describe the movement separately from the form, however, in terms of how it is abstracted to become the medium of a symbolic form, and the consequence of this abstraction.

In creating a dance, the dancer abstracts movement from its everyday occurrence and function in order that it may become aesthetically plastic, in order that it may be freely developed according to the demands of a symbolic form. The components of movement become qualities of virtual force the moment movement becomes aesthetically plastic, which is to say the moment the dancer begins working with the form. In the same way that there is no form in relation to dance which is not elaborated in movement, there is no movement in dance which is not formally elaborated. The transformation of the actual components of movement into qualities of virtual force occurs the moment the movement form or the formed movement is created. It is therefore clear that if movement is the medium of dance, such a medium does not exist apart from the dancer's creation of a form in the medium. This is because movement is abstracted from its everyday manifestations not as a specific symptomatic or referential expression of feeling, but as a medium of symbolic expression; yet not as a medium of symbolic expression which has concrete existence and awaits the touch of the dancer, but as a medium of symbolic expression which does not exist concretely except as these symbolic expressions are formed.[2] To describe movement in dance apart from the form is therefore to describe the difference between movement in everyday life and movement in dance; hence, the difference between symptomatic or referential expression of feeling and symbolic expression of feeling.

Movement in everyday life is commonly the means by which we express feelings: we jump for joy, fidget in boredom or impatience, open our arms in a gesture of fond greeting, and so on. All of these movements are symptomatic of our feelings. We move out our feelings in everyday life in ways which display or betray our feelings. The movement is a way of living the feeling directly and is thus an inherent mode of the feeling. Movement is not appended to the feeling as an afterthought or as a predetermined structure, but is spontaneous with the feeling itself. To speak of the movement as a symptom of the feeling is therefore not to separate the movement from the feeling as something existing separately from it, but rather to look at the movement as the feeling overtly expressed. For example, the "jump" for joy is part and parcel of the feeling so long as the feeling is a lived experience. As human beings, we all move out our feelings, and these movements, to an observer or to the person reflecting upon his own movements, are symptomatic of the feeling.

Movement is also referentially expressive of feeling in everyday life. For example, we wave good-bye in leaving someone, but the waving of hands is a socially and culturally derived expression of feeling. There is a difference in the way in which people of various cultures leave each other, and it is fortuitous that we

2. See Collingwood's notion that there is no pre-existing matter, no raw material, out of which the artistic form is made (*The Principles of Art*, New York, 1958, pp. 23–24).

use the particular movement we do in our society to show that we are going away. The movement refers to a feeling that we have, but is not intrinsically a part of that feeling except through social custom.

When movement is abstracted from everyday life, it is no longer a symptomatic or referential expression of feeling. We may use a previous example to illustrate this point. Shrugging one's shoulders in resignation was previously discussed as an example of how the sheer form of a feeling could be abstracted from an actual feeling. We may now consider this example not as a form of resignation, but as a movement which symptomatically expresses resignation, and which is consequently abstracted to become sheer movement.

The actual components of the movement are apparent: the shoulders are raised with a certain degree of intensity; the linear pattern of the movement is a vertical line; the movement is projected in a sustained manner until the shoulders reach their highest point; the downward movement of the shoulders is ballistic. The movement as a whole is a symptom of resignation and is the feeling of resignation insofar as it is felt as a "sigh" and a "giving in"; the raising of the shoulders is accompanied by an intake of breath and followed by a sudden release. When we abstract the sheer movement from the symptomatic expression, *we experience the movement and not the feeling,* just as when we abstracted the sheer form of the feeling we experienced the form and not the feeling. As sheer movement, the movement constitutes a form which may be elaborated. For example, one shoulder may rise and fall at a time; the shoulders may rise and fall together, but move from protraction to retraction instead of straight up and down, describing a circular rather than vertical linear pattern; the shoulders may be raised abruptly; the whole movement may be projected in a sustained and weak manner; etc. Furthermore, the movement need not be limited to movement of the shoulders. The arms may be raised sequentially with the shoulders; the head may drop to one side as the shoulders are released; or one might run forward as the shoulders are raised and stop abruptly as they are lowered. In short, the way in which the movement may be elaborated is unlimited. Finally, just as the sheer form was experienced as a revelation of force, so also is the sheer movement. Because form and movement are abstracted simultaneously, they are not actually separable but one and the same. One abstracts the form of human feelings from everyday life the moment one begins forming movement. And one abstracts movement from its affective context in everyday life the moment one begins creating a movement form. It may be noted again that if this abstracted movement constituted the beginning movement of a dance, the import of the dance would be embodied in and reflected by the totality of movement as a revelation of force. The import of the dance would not necessarily be approximated to resignation, and it could be approximated to a feeling having nothing to do with resignation at all.

   A final point may be made in reference to experiencing the form and the movement as a revelation of force. Since feelings in everyday life are commonly expressed in movement, it is consistent to speak of their form in terms of movement. Shrugging one's shoulders in resignation is a concise and simple example. The overt forms of human feelings in everyday life are, however, a great deal more complex than this, for all these overt forms take place within actual situational contexts and within a continuum of feeling. The implication, therefore, is not that the feeling of resignation is this simple and brief movement, and that after the movement is completed, one ceases to feel the resignation; thus, the form of resignation does not end with the movement. But the form may still be described in terms of body movement, in terms of the body's apparent and felt tension, in terms of the body's apparent and felt linear design, even if the person is motionless: as long as the feeling endures, a form of that feeling endures, and the bodily condition is still directly expressive of that form. Hence, the sheer form of a feeling is experienced as a revelation of force, even if no gestural expres-

sion is present: the dancer is moving even as she is "motionless."
The transformation of actual components of movement into
qualities of movement as a revelation of force is founded upon
the fact that movement is abstracted from its everyday context
to become expressive in a new context. Movement, through
abstraction, becomes plastic because it is no longer tied to actual
feelings or situations; it is free from any actual affective consciousness or practical everyday exigencies. Thus, it is clear why
the dancer is not "expressing herself" but rather, communicating forms of human feeling through a symbolic presentation.
The dancer is not symptomatically feeling feelings as she dances.
The kind of exhaustion which would come from such a venture
would far outweigh any natural fatigue that the dancer might
feel after performing. The dancer intuits her movement as a
perpetual revelation of sheer force which is spatially unified and
temporally continuous—as a sheer form-in-the-making. And her
intuition of the import of that form is the same as that of the
audience. If, for example, the form is symbolically expressive of a
form of love, the dancer perforce intuits this import as she
creates it through the form. Just as the audience is not feeling
love, neither is the dancer, because there is no love to feel.
Because the movement is abstracted from the symptomatic
expression of feeling in everyday life and because the sheer form
of feeling is abstracted from the actual feelings of everyday life,
no actual feeling is left. Only a sheer form-in-the-making is left,
a form which is symbolically expressive of a feeling.

There is one further aspect of abstraction to be considered in
relation to dance, for there are structural elements common to
any created form: variety, contrast, harmony, and the like.
These structural elements, however, do not exist in the symbolic
form of dance in the same way that the qualities of virtual force
exist: they have nothing to do with the elaboration or presentation of the form-in-the-making. They are apparent only upon
reflection, and are not immediately intuited with the form.

The particular interrelationship or organization of structural components within a form of actual feeling is a function of the affective consciousness; hence, the peaks of intensity within the form, its lulls, its quick propulsions, are not organized in an intentional manner, but are contingent upon the feeling as it is spontaneously felt by the affective consciousness. That the continuum of feeling in everyday life presents an orderly continuum of form is entirely fortuitous. The continuum of form may achieve a proportionate degree of variety, it may achieve balance, it may achieve a harmonious sequence, but it does not necessarily achieve such order. Why? Because the lived experience of actual feelings has nothing to do with a quest for formal variety, balance, and the like. One would have to look back upon forms of feeling in his life to note their balance, their climaxes, their contrasts; one cannot pre-arrange the continuum of form in any way so that these elements are present in an ordered manner and still *live* his experiences.

When the form of human feeling is abstracted from everyday life, it is freed from any and all exigencies of everyday life. Theoretically, its structural components may then be so organized as to yield an ordered form, wherein the lulls and suspensions are so organized that balance and harmony are present; wherein the total form, in brief, is developed to conform to "the principles of artistic composition." *But only theoretically.* For these principles of artistic composition have nothing to do with the development of the form. They are structural elements of a form *only after the form is completed,* and are apparent only as one reflects upon the form after it is presented. As "principles of composition," moreover, these structural elements are, in fact, afterthoughts of people viewing dance and not forethoughts of dancers engaged in creating dance.

When a dancer is engaged in creating a dance, she is working not with a conceptual form but a movement form. Obviously, it is only as movement is formed that a form is present. Hence, any attempt to work with variety, sequence, balance, or climax must be in vain, because such structural elements of form cannot exist in thin air. If they do exist, it is because the form-in-the-making exists. These structural elements are thus apparent only after one reflects upon the dance; they are not immediately created nor presented with the dance. They have to do with the way in which the form is built up, organized, arranged, but until the form is *created*, they do not exist. If one is to find instances of them in the form, one must stop the presentation of the form in order to find them, or reflect upon the form after it is presented. These elements are then determinable, analyzable structures of the form, but they have nothing to do with the lived experience of the form either as it is created or as it is presented.

These structural elements of form may not be "put into" a dance precisely because they exist outside it either as abstract concepts or as abstracted elements. "Repetition," for example, is an abstract concept, and it is also an element which may be abstracted from a particular dance. It is obvious that the form of a dance cannot incorporate "repetition" unless the abstract concept becomes a concrete element within the total form: unless an actual instance of repetition comes to exist within the total form-in-the-making. As an abstracted element, repetition may be found within the creation or presentation of a dance, but only insofar as one reflects upon the form, either as it is being created or presented, or after its creation or presentation. In the immediate intuition of dance, no such reflective thinking takes place, and if it does, it necessarily shatters the illusion which the dance creates.

It is evident, then, that until the form is created, the structural elements of form do not exist, and that when the form is created, the structural elements are apparent only upon reflection, only as they are abstracted from the total form. To be aware of their concrete exemplification in any particular dance is to be outside the lived experience of the dance. Hence, these structural elements are, at the most, conceptual anchors for our reflections upon dance. They are not "principles of composition," but perhaps categories for aesthetic evaluation. They cannot tell us anything about the *sense* of any particular dance, or about the *essence* of dance, but only how well the form of any particular dance meets individual aesthetic standards; individual in that what constitutes "balance" for one person will not necessarily constitute "balance" for another person, and in that these categories, by their very abstract nature, are made manifest by choreographers in a great variety of ways in different dances.

As conceptual anchors, these categories necessitate our looking at the form as an objective form: this movement phrase provides contrast in relation to that movement phrase; this section of the dance provides variety in relation to that section of the dance; this group of dancers is balanced by that group of dancers; and so on. What these categories describe, then, is the relative sense of order within any given form of dance. The form is looked upon as a progression of movement, rather than as a unified and continuous flow of force; it is a succession of movement phrases, sections, groupings, or what have you, which, as they are related to one another, either do or do not present an ordered form. Although one might be able to identify these structural elements within any given dance, and although they might be helpful in the criticism of dance, the basic criteria by which one evaluates dance should be directly related to the essence of dance and the sense of the particular dance. Perhaps a more lucid and vivid vocabulary of criticism would eventually emerge from a consideration of the phenomenal presence of dance as art.

In support of this suggestion, it may be noted that one cannot merely list the structural elements of form in the name of art: presumably, any well constructed artifact will have these attributes also. Yet more importantly, since these elements are already assumed to be attributes of "good" artistic form, or "good" art, their use in statements concerning art is often tautological: to say that the elements of form are inherent in all successful dances is equivalent to saying that the elements of form are the *sine qua non* of a good dance, a dance which utilizes the elements of form. Since they are structural elements of a form, but are apparent only as one abstracts them from an already completed form, they do not constitute the form of dance, or art, but rather, describe what some people hold to be common characteristics of "good" dance, or art.

We may now look more closely at what the dancer does work with in creating a symbolic form. She is working with abstracted movement and abstracted form, not as two distinct units, but as an inseparable unity. Abstracted movement lends itself to symbolic formulation because it is thereby made plastic, freed of any symptomatic or referential significance. It may be emphasized again, however, that until the very first movement of the dance is created, movement as the medium of dance does not exist. The form is then coincident with the movement as the movement is coincident with the form. They exist as one and the same thing as dance is created and presented: a sheer form-in-the-making.

The form-in-the-making is created through the interrelationship of the qualities of virtual force. The dancer is therefore working with qualitative aspects of the medium, tensional, linear, areal, and projectional qualities, not as distinct qualities, but as inter-dependent parts of a significant whole. The qualities are not and cannot be created singly, for movement perforce unites them all. Further, no quality exists before the movement is made, before the force is projected. Hence, the qualities are apparent only as the form is elaborated. But again it is necessary to distinguish between a reflective awareness of parts and a pre-reflective awareness of the whole. The qualities are apparent as the form is elaborated, but only reflectively apparent. They are immediately created and presented with the form, but they must be abstracted from the form in order to be described, reflected upon in and of themselves. The dancer's awareness is of the total movement as a revelation of force, and this total movement is not reducible to the particular qualities; as pointed out earlier, the qualities are neither additive nor discrete: one quality is not appended to another in the creation of the illusion, and no quality and no single movement reflects a meaning in and of itself.

If the qualities are singled out and worked with independently, the dancer's concern is to perfect the form or to grasp its development more clearly. The moment any quality is re-created or changed, an entirely new movement is created. For example, the moment the linear design of the body is altered, a new movement is created. The new linear design creates a new total configuration, a new *Gestalt*, not only because it has been changed, but because such a change has perforce influenced the other qualities, and hence the total movement. When the qualities are singled out they are actual components of movement, but they are actual components awaiting transformation, awaiting suffusion into the total form. They are grappled with actually in order to be fused symbolically with the form. One might, in fact, question whether the qualities are not sometimes singled out as actual components for the very reason that they already stand out as actual components; that is, they are noticed and recognized independently because they disturb the coherency of the form. We may recall the example in Chapter IV of "the single and flagrant line of the arm and hand" which interrupts the otherwise unified and continuous illusion of force.

To conclude this discussion of the inherent role of abstraction in the creation of a symbolic form, we may note that the dancer is working with form—the sheer form-in-the-making—and only form, and not with import, for import may only be reflected by the total form which is the dance. Abstraction provides the framework, so to speak, within which the dancer works to elaborate the form, and it is only through abstraction that the form of dance may be created and presented as a symbol.

CHAPTER VI

EXPRESSION

It has been maintained that abstraction functions to make what is real a virtual reality, and it is possible now to look at dance to see how expression accrues to the new form which is concrete in its own symbolic context.

A discussion of dance will often include three basic assumptions: (1) everyone accepts dance as an art form, (2) everyone accepts dance as being expressive, and expressive of something, and (3) everyone is agreed as to how these terms and variations of them qualify dance. On the basis of these assumptions, people may speak of the aesthetic or expressive nature of dance without ever describing what they mean by "aesthetic" or "expressive." They might begin by saying, "Dance is an aesthetic activity which . . . ," or "Dance is an expressive activity which . . . ," and go on from there to describe dance. Since there is obviously something in dance which makes it aesthetic and expressive, we are thus led back to the original question, What is dance? Any complete answer to that question will necessarily include some elaboration of dance as an expressive form, and specifically, as an expressive art form.

In concordance with Mrs. Langer, we have already seen how the illusion created in dance is virtual force, and how this descriptive analogue is both lucid and significant: phenomenologically, dance does create an illusion of force in the appearance of moving forces which are seen not as actual concrete body movements of everyday life, but as virtual forces emanating from the dancer's body. In fact, the moment concentration is focused upon the actual physical body, and not the movement, the dance disappears. What is left is the perception of an arm moving sideways, a flexed spine, etc. But by the same token, neither can one look at the movement and call it dance. For if one concentrates on the movement as movement, either analytically or synthetically, remarking, for example, "The line of that movement is awful," or "What a fine leap!" then the dance is no longer there either. Only when we give ourselves to what is being presented, wholly and unequivocally, neither analyzing nor judging, but intuiting what is going on as a *Gestalt*, separating neither the body from the movement nor the movement from the dance, do we see the form which sustains the illusion.

But what, after all, is this form besides being a sheer form? In what way is it expressive? To explicate fully the nature of expression in dance we must clarify the nature of dance as symbol beyond the necessary "logical congruity of forms" which Mrs. Langer has specified and which we have described, in relation both to the body itself, and to body movement. We must look at the symbol of dance itself, determine what it is, and what is the foundation of its being.

A symbol has a concrete form and a meaning of some order which are created, presented, and intuited concurrently. The meaning aspect of the symbol does not exist apart from the concrete form which embodies and reflects it; and conversely, the concrete form does not exist apart from the meaning it reflects. If dance is a symbol, and if dance, while being something more than the phenomenon of body movement is nothing less than the phenomenon of body movement, it is clearly that basic phenomenon which must be described in relation to the symbolic nature of dance.

Movement in dance is peculiar in that it neither signifies something otherwise designatable, nor is any particular movement in the dance a symbol in and of itself. This seeming inability to describe a single movement is adducible to the fact that one can speak of movement either as the vehicle through which a form is presented, or as the form-in-the-making itself. But if movement is looked at separately from the form as a medium, the dance disappears. As noted earlier, if concentration is upon movement *qua* movement, what we are left with is a series of movements all out of context with each other and with the total dance. Thus, it is clear why movement *qua* movement in dance is not expressive at all, except as it is read as a conventionally fixed sign of something. The movements of a dance, as abstracted from everyday feeling patterns, become functional parts of an expressive symbol: they are symbolically expressive only as they relate to each other within the total form-in-the-making. It thus becomes apparent why there is no division between the sheer form and what it expresses, either in the creation, presentation, or intuition of dance: the unitary nature of the form and its import derives from the fact that movement in dance does not exist apart from its appearance as a sheer form-in-the-making. It is created, presented, and intuited as a perpetual revelation of sheer force, which is internally unified and continuous, and which cannot be reduced to separate and particular meanings. It is because movement is so created, presented, and intuited that the symbol which is dance comes to be.

By the very nature of its wholeness, the symbol is a single and

distinctive phenomenon: what is expressed is a cohesive meaning reflected by a presentationally cohesive form. This being so,
each unique revelation of force within any given dance is not
only integral to, but the foundation of, each dance's being the
particular expressive symbol which it is. As Cassirer states in the
Philosophy of Symbolic Forms, symbols are:

. . . the totality of those phenomena in which the sensuous is
in any way filled with meaning, in which a sensuous content,
while preserving the mode of its existence and facticity, represents
a particularization and embodiment, a manifestation and in-
carnation of a meaning.[1]

The sheer form-in-the-making is a sensuous surface, a unified
multiplicity of movement, which transcends its facticity insofar
as it reflects a unique meaning. Yet it is the very facticity of each
particular form-in-the-making which is the basis for its uniqueness: the movement by which each form comes to exist is the
foundation for its being the form which it is. Although each
movement in a dance is not created as a discrete movement, it is
the specificity of each movement as a particular revelation of
force which makes the dance singularly distinctive, both in
terms of its completeness and its meaning. It is in this sense that
the form-in-the-making preserves "the mode of its existence and
facticity."

To illustrate this phenomenological fact, we may suppose that
within the context of a dance, a dancer runs from the upstage
left corner to the downstage right corner. The movement as a
revelation of sheer force has an extensive areal pattern, and it is
projected in a straight line. Yet beyond this, the movement has

1. Ernst Cassirer, *Philosophy of Symbolic Forms* (New Haven, 1953),
III, p. 93. Cassirer's use of the phrase "sensuous content" refers to the
sensuous actuality of the phenomenon, its actual physical and concrete
presence. The term "content" may therefore be misleading to the effect
that there is first a thing, a phenomenon, and secondly a content which
it holds, and thirdly a meaning which the content reflects. The phenomenon, on the contrary, is the content and the meaning. The term "surface"
will be used to avoid any ambiguity.

either a relatively constant, or a changing, tensional and projectional quality, and the body has either a relatively constant, or a changing, linear and areal design. If the linear and areal designs of the body change as the run is executed, the tensional and projectional qualities perforce also change, and vice versa. The run may begin with the body in a compact areal design and may end in an expansive design; it may begin vigorously and end in a subdued manner; it may begin with a diagonal linear design of the body and end in a vertical design; and so on, to an infinite number of qualitative possibilities within the total movement. In sum, the qualitative variables in any given movement are manifold, and it is precisely the specificity of each movement as a particular revelation of force which pulls them together, thus making the movement a constant within the total dance: the run is uniquely characterized as being this particular run and none other. This specificity of movement is the foundation of each dance's being a singularly distinctive whole reflecting a singularly distinctive meaning.

It is therefore clear that while movement in dance has no meaning apart from its appearance as a sheer form-in-the-making, it is the foundation of the meaning engendered in that sheer form. If the sensuous surface were not an internally unified and continuous multiplicity of movement, but an externally related series of movements, the surface would be something akin to a mold into which movement were poured; each movement would be a separate and specific content of the form-in-the-making. As such, a determination of what is expressed would not only be a matter of relating specific meanings to specific movements, it would also be a matter of reducing the meaning of any dance to a sum of particular and absolute meanings. On the contrary, because what is expressed is irreducible, the sheer form and its import are created, presented, and intuited simultaneously. And furthermore, they mutually determine one another: the meaning aspect of the symbol derives from the specific sensuous surface which embodies and reflects it, and the sensuous surface is the *sine qua non* of the specific meaning reflected.

If the import of any particular dance is not something conferred upon the dance nor something which appears piecemeal, if the dance in and of itself reflects import, it is the sheer form of the dance which is expressive. Because the form is symbolically expressive of human feeling, the import of the dance is an expressive meaning which pertains to or relates to feelings, such as the pure phenomenon of anguish, love, or fear. This fact was amply described in the previous chapter. The question which confronts us here is, How does the sheer form become symbolically expressive such that a pure phenomenon of feeling is reflected? If all dances are *inherently* expressive, if each inherently reflects a unique meaning, an import, which relates to feelings, the nature of movement must be clarified further in relation to that unique meaning: movement as a perpetual revelation of sheer force must be such that it characterizes the expressive nature of the form. Again, as Cassirer points out in his phenomenological account of expressive forms,

Where the "meaning" or the world is still taken as that of pure expression, every phenomenon discloses a definite "character," which is not merely deduced or inferred from it but which belongs to it immediately. It is in itself gloomy or joyful, agitating or soothing, pacifying or terrifying. These determinations are expressive values and factors adhering to the phenomena themselves; they are not merely derived from them indirectly by way of the subjects which we regard as standing behind the phenomenon. It is a misunderstanding of the phenomena of pure expression when a certain psychological theory makes them originate in a secondary act of interpretation and declares them to be products of "empathy." [2]

What this means is that the sheer form of dance, as pure expression, is in and of itself gloomy or joyful, agitating or soothing, etc. It means that we, as audience, do not feel gloomy,

2. Cassirer, *Philosophy of Symbolic Forms*, p. 72.

joyful, or whatever. We do not interpret the dance on the stage
in terms of feelings it might evoke in us and then confer upon
the dance that meaning. We do not feel tensions and strains and
interpret these as representing a certain feeling quality to be
attributed to the dance. When we look at a dance we see a form
which, because of its very organization, its very dynamic
flow—the way forces are released, checked, attenuated, so-
lidified, diffused—is symbolically expressing a feeling. The very
specific dynamic flow of a dance, the very specific qualitative
organization of force, makes the dance in and of itself "gloomy"
or "joyful," although even these attempts at verbal designation
of feeling must be considered only as approximations. As
pointed out earlier, the lived experience of the dance is not
reducible to verbal equivalents or verbal descriptions. The most
we can say is that the sheer form of a dance is in and of itself
expressive of a pure phenomenon of feeling. And the most we
can do is describe how, in Cassirer's words, the expressive "character" of the phenomenon of a given dance is embodied in its
form.

What makes each dance uniquely significant is the *dynamics*
of the form; hence, the unique interplay of qualities inherent in
movement as a perpetual revelation of sheer force. The dynamic
organization of the form—attenuations, diffusions, potencies,
quicknesses, slownesses, verticalities, amplitudes—is the way in
which movement as a revelation of force—*sheer force*—spatializes and temporalizes itself. A revelation is something heretofore not revealed. Consequently, not only force itself, but also
space and time, are perpetually created. The dynamics of the
form are therefore created by the nature of the forces themselves, tensional qualities, and by the manner in which those
forces spatialize and temporalize themselves: linear, areal, and
projectional qualities. The qualitative interrelationships created
by movement as a revelation of sheer force create the dynamics,
and the dynamics, in turn, create the particular expressive
character of the dance.

To summarize, we may say that the expressive form is a symbolic form by virtue of its logical congruity with forms of actual feeling, and by virtue of the import it reflects in and of itself through its organized sensuous surface. We may add to this phenomenological description by pointing out that the import of the expressive form, through its sheer dynamic organization, is related to feeling. We intuit the sheer dynamic form and feeling concurrently; at the moment of intuition, the two cannot be separated. Furthermore, the one determines the other: they are interdependent. What may characterize the symbolic nature of the expressive form as aesthetic is that the form does not express feeling symptomatically or referentially, but is expressive of forms of feeling. What may characterize the expressive nature of the symbolic form as aesthetic is that the form reflects an expressive meaning, an import, in and of itself, and it has no meaning beyond the import it reflects. Unlike other expressive forms, for example, a fire, or a waterfall, the expressive form of dance has no significance beyond its inherent, self-contained meaning. The aesthetic nature of the form comes not from its being a mere organized sensuous surface, a mere pattern of movements, but from its being a created form which, through its very unique dynamic organization, embodies and reflects a symbolically expressive meaning, a meaning which begins and ends with the dance.

In describing the nature of expression in dance, we have come full circle in the description of dance as it is immanently present to consciousness. Dance, as a symbol of the form of human feelings, immediately creates and sustains an illusion of force. That global phenomenon, that total and perpetual creation of sheer force, is expressive of a pure phenomenon of feeling by virtue of the dynamic structure inherent in the symbolic form of the dance. The dynamics of the symbolic form, in turn, are created by the qualitative interrelationships inherent in movement as a revelation of sheer force. It is thus the qualitative nature and structure of movement as a revelation of sheer force which is the foundation of the unique illusion which any dance creates and the pure phenomenon of feeling which it reflects. Whether one speaks of the expressive nature of the symbol, or the expressive nature of the illusion, it is understood that it is the latter which is the global phenomenon and the former which is its foundational or underlying structure: the symbolic form of dance is expressive, but that symbolic form exists within the totally differentiated modality of the illusion which all dance creates, and which each dance creates uniquely.

Rather than stopping at this explication of how movement as a revelation of force is the foundation of the expressive symbol and the symbolic expression, we may look further in order to discover how the dynamics of the symbolically expressive form relate to composition, for we have not as yet fully described the dance as it is created; specifically, the structures inherent in the creation of a pure dynamic form. It is only through such further analysis that we can describe how the form comes to be in and of itself expressive of a pure phenomenon of feeling, how the "character" of the dance comes to belong to the dance itself.

CHAPTER VII

DYNAMIC LINE

Our task now is actually to elucidate the process of composition in light of what we know about dance, for everything which has been descriptive of the dance relates to the concrete thing which in fact has been created: a dance composition. Since the illusion of force which dance creates is founded upon a symbolic moving form, a sheer form-in-the-making, and is thus contingent upon the simultaneous abstractions of both form and movement from everyday life, the nature of the illusion of force has been described in relation to the actual components of movement being transformed into qualities of virtual force, qualities whose very unique inter-relatedness in movement make the form uniquely dynamic, creating a particular illusion of force expressive of a particular and pure phenomenon of feeling. But apart from the necessary abstractions which are basic to the creation of the illusion, or symbol, the illusion of force as it appears has also been described as spatially unified and temporally continuous. The spatial and temporal structures of the illusion of force are intrinsic to the totality of that force. Yet not only do the structures have no existence apart from the whole, they also have no existence apart from each other: there is no spatiality without temporality and no temporality without spatiality. Temporality and spatiality are bound to one another, in the same way that the qualities through which they are made apparent are bound to one another, in and through movement. Such a notion was mentioned in Chapter II in speaking of the manner in which space and time are apprehended: one cannot be pre-reflectively aware of his spatiality and at the same time be reflectively aware of his temporality. To consider spatiality and temporality separately is not to suggest that they actually exist apart from each other, or apart from the unified and continuous whole in which they inhere; rather, it is to understand better the manner of their creation in the total form of the dance.

In order to describe the dynamic structure of the illusion of force, we must necessarily be concerned with a further description of the time and space of dance; specifically, the created spatiality and temporality of the illusion of force in relation to the qualitative structure of that force. The spatial and temporal structures must be analyzed further because their inherence in the creation of the illusion was described only in terms of the fact that movement of the body as a revelation of force is apprehended by dancer and audience alike as a sheer form-in-the-making. But what of the revelation of force itself? As was noted in the previous chapter, it is the very organization of forces—the way in which the qualities of force temporalize and spatialize force—which makes the form uniquely dynamic and expressive. Thus, we may ask, What is there in the form which allows the composing dancer to apprehend its dynamics and how does she do this?

A choreographer strives for and is aware of a unity and continuity of form. She chooses one movement and not another; she may change any qualitative aspect of a movement in order to perfect the form. What is the basis for the choice or change? Why, on the basis of the oft heard statement, "It feels right," is the one movement chosen or the change made? Is there something which guides the choreographer in the development of the form? To speak of a guide is not to imply that it is thereby possible to teach dancers how to compose, but only to affirm that it is possible to make them aware of something substantial, something which is there in the finished dance and only awaits exploration and clarification in terms of composition.

Movement as a perpetual revelation of force creates a dynamic line. This is not an actual line, but "line" in the sense of an on-going projection of forces from a beginning point. Each dance creates its own dynamic line, a unique qualitative organization of forces from beginning to end. In each revelation of force a specific tensional quality is projected in a specific qualitative manner. Thus, the basis for the *flow* of force in dance, its dynamic line, is projectional and tensional quality: a sheer force of whatever potency is qualitatively projected, and the manner of its projection will govern its temporality. Take, for example, the temporalization of a particular force in an abrupt flexion of the elbow, a full body swing, or a sustained extension of the leg; each movement as a revelation of force creates its own temporality by virtue of the manner in which it is projected. Each of these movements creates a specific temporal flow of force according to the potency of the force and the manner in which it is released. A qualitative interrelationship is born.

Yet each projection creates not only a unique temporality, but also a unique spatiality. An abrupt flexion of the elbow, a full body swing, or an extension of the leg is a projection of force which uniquely spatializes itself as it is projected. But unlike the temporality created by any projection of force, the spatiality is describable in terms other than projection and tension; namely, line and area. For the spatiality created by any projection of force has to do not only with the *manner* in which space is created, but with the projected designs and patterns as well. It is precisely because each projection of force creates its own space as it creates its own time that the dynamic line of movement is spatially unified as it is temporally continuous. The linear and areal qualities created in all projections of force, relate to the *unified* spatiality of the body or bodies as centers of force, and of body movement as projected force. The qualitative interrelationship is then fully realized in the dynamic line *inherent* in movement as a revelation of force.

The dynamic line which movement creates may be mirrored by a vocalized or inwardly heard dynamic line. Although frequently used in dance, the vocalized dynamic line has been described neither in itself, nor in relation to the dynamic line of movement which it reflects. Yet such descriptions would appear to be essential. Not that choreographers and dancers, students and teachers of dance cannot continue to use a vocalized dynamic line effectively until it has been carefully explained and evaluated; obviously, it is utilized because it is already meaningful: it is an effective means of making clear and reinforcing the dynamic line of the movement. But how? And why?

The first two syllables of "Baa Baa Black Sheep" are the kinds of syllables one might utter in vocalizing the dynamic line of any created movement, for the vocalized line is not intended to be verbally meaningful. A brief descriptive analysis of the usual and various ways in which these syllables are and might be uttered in the nursery rhyme, will be indicative of the qualitative possibilities apparent in any vocalized dynamic line.

Most commonly, the vocal intensity of each "baa" is moderately strong; the force of utterance is neither vigorous nor weak. Neither is each syllable abrupt nor abruptly cut off, but rather, the two are almost merged. If we take these two syllables and make their intensity more potent, we can feel the stronger tension in the throat: the breath, instead of being exhaled in a semi-relaxed manner is, on the contrary, forcefully expelled. If the two syllables are projected abruptly, the vowel sound is cut short, the emphasis put on the consonant. We can make the two changes in utterance simultaneously and come up with a vigorous and explosive Baa! Baa!, or perhaps better written, Bah! Bah! We can keep the first syllable as it is usually uttered and change the second one, or vice versa; we can inhale as we utter the second syllable and either attenuate its projection or make it rise abruptly; in short, we can make all manner of gradation in *intensity* and *projection*.

The vocalized dynamic line thus encompasses two of the qualities which movement encompasses bodily as a revelation of force: tensional quality and projectional quality. It indicates tensional quality through the intensity of the vocalized syllable, projectional quality through the manner in which the air forming the syllable is taken in and expelled. The tensional and projectional qualities of the vocalized dynamic line will thus mirror the tensional and projectional qualities of movement, the dynamic line inherent and immediately apparent in the movement form. The vocalized dynamic line, in effect, mirrors the created time of the dance and thus its temporal continuity, for the flow of vocal force is founded, too, upon the created temporality inherent in any kinetic phenomenon, in any projection of force.

If we take a simple movement of the arm, abduction to shoulder height and adduction back to the side of the body, and use the aforementioned syllables in their usual manner of utterance to duplicate the tensional and projectional qualities of the movement, it is apparent that the dynamics of the movement are reflected and reinforced by the vocalized dynamic line: the two movements are executed with the same moderately strong tensional quality and the same even projection, even to the point that they, too, tend to have no clear cut separation. If we utter the syllables vigorously and explosively, Bah! Bah!, the movement is similarly vigorous and explosive.

The above examples actually illustrate movement as mirror of a vocalized dynamic line. A vocalized dynamic line as mirror of the dynamic line of movement is created in an exactly converse manner. The examples have been given in reverse only in order to simplify the illustration. The dynamic line of the movement is necessarily of far greater significance, for the vocalized line is no more than an adjunctive tool by which the dancer may grasp more clearly the unity and continuity of the form, the actual dynamic line of the movement. The prime significance of the dynamic line of movement is also apparent in the fact that the dancer will usually set forth her original idea in movement and not in a vocalized line. Thus, if the same abduction and adduction of the arm were taken as a starting point, it is apparent that whatever characterizes the tensional and projectional qualities of those movements may be recognized and reinforced through a vocalization of the dynamic line. If the abduction is weak and sustained, the adduction strong and abrupt, the vocalized line which mirrors the movement might be written as: baaaaaaaaaaaaaaaaaaaaaaaaaaaaaaa-BAH! If a sustained and strong abduction and an abrupt and weak adduction: BAAAAAAAAAAAAAAAAAAAAAA-bah.

A dynamic line may be vocalized first and movement subsequently created which mirrors the line, or movement may be created first and the line reflecting the movement subsequently vocalized. It is thoroughly possible that the line be inwardly heard simultaneously as the movement is created, or that as one vocalizes a line, he envisions movement which embodies that line. The important point, in fact, is that *the vocalization and the movement are ultimately executed and apprehended together; phenomenologically, they constitute one and the same projection and intuition.*

Since the breathing mechanism underlies the vocalization of

syllables, its importance to an awareness of dynamic line may be noted. Breathing is usually relatively even and unchanging rather than dynamic; there are, in a "normal" state, no great variations in the way the breath is inhaled or exhaled. However, such variations or changes may occur through conscious effort. Nonetheless, these changes can only occur to a limited extent in terms of tensional and projectional qualities. Much greater latitude in tensional quality may come about through a vocalized syllable which, by its range of loudness or softness, for example, may indicate a wider gamut of intensity. Likewise, much greater latitude in the manner of projection of force is possible in that the physiological demands of breathing are not dominant: the movement is not limited by the fact that one does not have any more air to exhale or can no longer inhale. A syllable may, in other words, be projected over the breathing. Breathing, however, is the basis for the vocalized dynamic line: it engenders both tensional and projectional qualities. To vocalize a very specific flow of force necessitates a very specific manner of breath control. It may be recalled that to shrug the shoulders in resignation, one inhales as the shoulders are raised, and exhales as they are lowered; the inhalation and exhalation control the desired flow of force which symptomatically expresses resignation.

If the dynamic line of the movement is descriptive of the inherent dynamic flow of the sheer form being created, and if the vocalized line is an adjunctive tool through which the composing dancer is able to grasp the flow more clearly, a valid question arises: Is there only one movement which correctly follows a previous movement? Can a specific but incomplete dynamic line hold many future possibilities? To use a vocal example, if "Baa Baa Black Sheep" were vocalized using only the syllables "baa baa," and if one stopped vocalizing upon reaching "any," it is apparent that many future possibilities would exist. For example, the dynamic line would still flow

logically, apart from any recitative meaning, if one would repeat
"have you any" twice, then vocalize "wool." Thus,

Baa Baa Black Sheep have you any have you any have you any wool
Ba ba Ba ba Bababa Bababa Bababa Ba

One might therefore answer that a dynamic line may call
forth a variety of movements, but within the context of a specific
dance composition, only one logical flow of movement exists,
just as within the context of this particular child's verse only one
logical flow exists. According to the context and accrued formal
import at any point in the compositional process, a specific
logical flow of movement is to be found. The dancer must search
out the logical formal future of any given movement. Tacit in
such a conception of dynamic line is the emphasis upon the
movement itself, where it wants to go: the dance as an expressive
art form must exist as a thing formally apart from the personal
predilections of the dancer. The dancer, of course, controls her
materials, but the control in the end is unseen or seen only as a
function of the movement itself. Through the use of a vocalized
dynamic line, the dancer becomes increasingly and more keenly
aware of the dynamic flow of movement, the unity and continuity of each revelation of force in terms of the total form. Thus,
the inclusion of extraneous movement is obviated, movement
which one simply likes to do, movement which one includes
because one does it well, etc. To develop the form is to create a
dynamic line of sheer force which is logically consistent with all
that has gone before and all that will come to be. But the dancer
is aware of the logical consistency of the form only insofar as she
is aware of the unity and continuity of the dynamic line which
she is creating; hence, the helpfulness of the adjunctive vocalized line. It would seem that it is not only feasible but desirable
that a dancer be able to vocalize her dance from beginning to end.

If the dynamic line of movement is founded upon the
qualitative organization and flow of force in dance, and if that

line may be apprehended through vocalization, two further questions must be answered. The first of these may be stated as follows: Since the vocalized dynamic line has only two of the four qualities of force, tensional and projectional qualities, in what way may it be said to mirror the totality of that force? What about the linear and areal qualities?

Since the tensional and projectional qualities relate to the potency of the force projected and the manner of its projection, it is apparent that they control almost entirely the linear and areal qualities. For example, if the arm is abruptly and strongly abducted, the particular degree of abruptness and strength will govern the linear and areal designs and patterns created by the movement. The tensional and projectional qualities will govern the linear design of the body, the degree to which the arm attains a horizontality in relation to the verticality of the body; they will govern also the linear pattern of the moving arm, the length of the line of the arc made by the tips of the fingers; and finally, they will determine the compactness or amplitude of both the areal design of the body and the areal pattern of the movement. The linear and areal qualities cannot exceed or fall short of the limits set by the particular potency of force or by the particular manner of its projection.

Even if a linear and areal quality is stipulated in advance, if, for example, abduction of the arm is taken to mean abduction to shoulder level, the tensional and projectional qualities of the movement will still engender the linear and areal qualities, and they will control these to the degree that they coincide exactly with the designated movement, or rather, that they allow this movement to occur. There is, in other words, no spatialization of force apart from the projection of force which creates the desired spatiality.

One mode of "stipulation," however, might be seen as governing tensional and projectional qualities, and this mode has to do with the linear and areal design of the body. If one would stipulate that the abduction be made with the elbow flexed so that the forearm and upper arm formed a "v," the fingertips approximating the shoulders, the areal and linear qualities would obviously be curtailed because of anatomical limitations. To abduct the arm in this position would really be to abduct only the upper arm so that the range of movement and the extent of the arc drawn by the tip of the elbow would be limited. To abduct the arm abruptly and vigorously with this particular linear and areal design would be to create not only a linear and areal quality very different from the original example, but a different tensional and projectional quality as well.

Tensional and projectional qualities are, then, governed to some extent by the linear and areal design of the body; the particular potency of force to be projected is limited to the gamut of force possible from a given position, and the projection of force is limited to the manner in which force can be projected from a given position; for example, with the arm in a "v" position, a free swing is impossible. The tensional and projectional qualities, in short, cannot exceed the anatomical limitations of the body. Even so, it is again clear that as soon as the tensional and projectional qualities of the abductive movement are created, a particular spatialization of force is immediately created: *linear and areal qualities are inherent and immediately apparent in any projection of force.*

The reason for noting this apparent limiting of tensional and projectional qualities by the body's areal and linear design is to bring the discussion of dynamic line as close as possible to the process of composition. Where the dancer may go at any point in the development of the form is governed by the present linear and areal design of the body. The anatomical relationships at any given moment may be seen, however, not so much as limiting but as affecting the consequent flow of force. The design of the body at any moment in the composition is part of the total flow of force to that point; the body has arrived at a given design because of the demands of the form, because of the logical development of the dynamic line. If the concentration is on the dynamic line, and not on the position and "how to get out of it," the consequent created movement will be integrally related to what has gone before: it will extend the unity and continuity of the form. Hence, the significance of the vocalized dynamic line which allows the dancer to concentrate on the dynamics of the form rather than on particular qualitative aspects of that form—really actual components—or particular points and moments of it.

To speak of the tensional and projectional qualities of movement as governing its linear and areal qualities is not to imply that the spatialization of force is subordinate to, or a function of, the temporalization of force, but only to affirm that there is no spatialization of force without the projection of force itself. Once the projection is created, particular linear and areal qualities are immediately created. It becomes clear, then, that the vocalized dynamic line figuratively creates a particular spatiality while the dynamic line of movement literally does. The intensity of a syllable and the manner in which it is uttered reflect the linear and areal qualities of movement insofar as they are a concurrent replication of the dynamic line of the movement. Because the vocalized line does not exist apart from the movement, and because it is an exact verbal rendering of the movement as a revelation of force, it perforce reflects the space which the movement creates: *this particular linear quality and this particular areal quality and none other.*

But how, one may ask, it is possible for the dancer to be aware of both of these dynamic lines simultaneously, and furthermore, how may she exist her body in movement as a sheer form-in-the-making if she is concerned with dynamic line at all? It was pointed out in Chapter III that because the dancer is pre-reflectively aware of her body in movement as a sheer form-in-the-making, she is able to spatialize and temporalize the form such that it exists *ekstatically* and diasporatically. What, then, is the meaning of the dynamic line in terms of this pre-reflective awareness? Moreover, it may be asked how someone can be pre-reflectively aware of the sheer flow of force if that flow is being explicitly duplicated through actual vocalization. This second question about dynamic line relates to the dance as it is being both composed and performed.

Since the dancer is pre-reflectively aware of movement as a *sheer* form-in-the-making, her pre-reflective awareness of the form is an awareness of its pure dynamic flow; hence, it is an awareness of the dynamic line of the movement, its total qualitative structure. Through such awareness the dancer is able to create and apprehend the totality and vibrancy of the form, something of no given moments or points, but which continually pulsates, which perpetually flows and is revealed: in brief, something which exists *ekstatically* and diasporatically.

It is therefore evident that in terms of composition, the dancer's awareness of the dynamic line will govern almost exclusively the unity and continuity of the form she is creating. The dance as a symbol of the form of human feeling makes the dynamic flow of any specific form of paramount significance; the way forces are checked, released, gathered together, dispersed; their potency, their quickness; all qualitative aspects of the flow will create a particular and unique form, and hence also, a particular and unique import. To achieve a unity and continuity of form which does, in fact, express a pure phenomenon of feeling, the dancer must be aware of the pure dynamic flow of forces which constitute the form and make it a unique symbolic expression.

The dancer's pre-reflective awareness of the vocalized dynamic line does not exist apart from her awareness of the dynamic line of the movement, whether the line is actually vocalized or whether it is inwardly heard: insofar as the dancer is pre-reflectively aware of the vocalized line, that line is immediately created and apprehended with the movement and is inseparable from the movement. It is in reflection that the vocalized line exists apart from the movement. As the dancer reflects upon the line, she may be contemplating it in order to grasp its future more readily, or in order to perfect the dynamic flow of the form already created. The dynamic line, when reflectively grasped, is a critical tool in the making of compositions; it gives the composing dancer a clear insight into the logicality of the form through a concrete delineation of its dynamic flow.

There are several points which may be mentioned here in connection with a reflective awareness of dynamic line. The first of these is that an awareness of dynamic line does not and cannot guarantee a dance. Thus, the above qualification, "dynamic line will govern *almost exclusively.* . . ." There are no rules which someone may follow as a recipe in the hope of creating a dance. There are only tools, so to speak, and these tools derive from the nature and experience of dance itself. Secondly, these tools are valid only to the extent that the dancer working with them becomes sensitive to them; they are not facile techniques. The mere awareness of a dynamic line will not insure the dancer's ability to be guided by it, nor will it insure any depth of sensitivity. Finally, a logical flow of form is something which only the individual composer can establish; taking the same beginning movement, two dancers will come up with two entirely unique dances. For example, if the beginning movement is a sustained and weak flexion of the neck with a sustained and weak raising of the arms, the movement which flows from this beginning will immediately call forth a particular logical development for each individual dancer. It is like a single chord on the piano which is not limited to a single future: it is a "free" chord which has many future possibilities.

The composing dancer may be either pre-reflectively or reflectively aware of the dynamic line, depending upon whether her purpose is to rehearse the dance as a performance, or to evaluate the form as she composes. The performing dancer, on the other hand, may only be pre-reflectively aware of the dynamic line, for the reasons elaborated in Chapter III: if there is a separation of the dancer from the dance, the illusion of force is destroyed. The performing dancer does not actually vocalize the dynamic line—although presumably she could—but inwardly "hears" the dynamic line as she simultaneously projects her movement as a dynamic flow of force, and thereby intuits its unity and continuity. Furthermore, since she is the center of force, it is apparent that she neither lags behind nor anticipates the flow, for in doing so she would be *reflectively* concentrated at a moment or point behind or ahead of the dance. Rather, she is the flow itself. The flow is the momentless and pointless revelation of force, and to be that flow, the dancer must always be present with it. The dynamic line which is a unique flow of sheer force immanently present to consciousness is what makes the dancer inseparable from the dance. Her pre-reflective awareness of the dynamic line is an awareness of the pure dynamics of the form being presented and the pure phenomenon of feeling that dynamic form expresses; it is a lived experience of the dance.

Because a dancer, as she is creatively engaged in the making of a dance, is perforce creating a unique dynamic structure, it becomes abundantly clear why the dynamic line which movement creates is of supreme importance, and how and why a vocalization of the dynamic line is an effective means of making clear and reinforcing one's awareness of the qualitative flow of movement. Through a description of the nature of a vocalized line, in itself, and in relation to the dynamic line of movement which it reflects, we can also understand why it is already utilized as a meaningful adjunctive tool.

While this chapter has shown how the dynamic line of movement is founded upon all the qualities of virtual force, it has not fully elucidated how the interrelationship of qualities creates a unified and continuous flow of force; specifically, how the qualities of force relate to the temporal flow of force, and how they create intensities within that flow. The aim of the following chapter will therefore be to clarify further the nature of dynamic line, and to seek out a phenomenological concept of rhythm on the basis of the qualitative changes apparent in the temporal flow of force.

CHAPTER VIII

MORE ON DYNAMIC LINE:
A PHENOMENOLOGICAL
CONCEPT OF RHYTHM

Rhythm, like everything which relates to dance, does not exist until a dance exists. To advance a definition of rhythm prior to a determination of what dance is, is to look at dance as already possessing the characteristics to be noted: an ebb and flow, for example, or a time-force relationship. Let us rather begin by looking again at the phenomenon in question, at dance, the creation of virtual force. Our concern will be to explicate further the qualitative aspects of virtual force in the hope of clarifying the nature of rhythm in dance. The only assumption is that there may be something in dance which may be called rhythm, but the nature of that something is not predetermined.

The projectional quality of force, as described earlier, is apparent in the manner in which force is released. It was also pointed out that the general designations of projectional quality as abrupt, sustained, or ballistic were actually inclusive of a range of gradations within the particular quality. An example of this range in everyday life might be the infinite number of degrees of abruptness possible in slamming a door. Furthermore, prior to its closing, the door may be fully opened so that it almost forms a straight line with the open doorway, or it may be partially closed to any degree from that maximal position. If it is slammed abruptly from a maximal opened position, the abruptness of its closing is elongated; if it is opened minimally, the abruptness of its closing is shortened. But the degree of abruptness is still variable regardless of the distance. Thus, in relation to movement of the human body, if an arm is extended and abducted at shoulder height and is brought down to the side of the body abruptly, the abruptness of the movement is elongated; if the arm is at a minimal distance from the side of the body and is abruptly brought to the side, the abruptness of the movement is shortened. But again, the degree of abruptness of movement is still variable regardless of the distance separating the arm from the side of the body. It is therefore evident that as soon as a particular projectional quality is created, a specific temporality is thereby created. But it is also evident that the range of the body and the movement, the areal quality, affects the temporality of the movement. If the arm is in an abducted position at shoulder height and is brought down abruptly to the side of the body, the abruptness is prolonged in relation to a less abducted arm, so long as the degree of abruptness is constant. However, if there is no desire to compare temporality, neither can there be a consideration of areal quality as governing temporality. But areal quality does affect temporality, in the same way that projectional and tensional qualities affect spatiality, as described in the previous chapter: each movement in a dance is unique and absolute in terms of its qualitative structure. Areal quality affects the temporality of a movement insofar as a beginning and an end position are chosen in advance; but until the actual movement is made, until a particular projection of force is created and revealed which unites the beginning and end positions, the particular temporality of the movement is not created. Areal quality also affects the temporality of a movement insofar as the mere beginning position is established. What will determine the end position is the very temporality of the projected force itself.

At any moment in composing the form, the dancer may either decide in advance where she wants to move, or the movement may be freely developed with no predetermined end point. In either situation, the temporality of the movement is controlled by the temporality of the particular projection of force, and it is affected by the areal quality to the extent that any projection of force is affected by the range of its projection. The temporality of the flight of a ball through the air is governed by the thrust, by the force with which it is projected, and the manner of its projection; the areal quality, the range of the flight, affects the temporality of the flight but does not control it.

Consequently, one can speak of the specific temporal flow of a specific movement and the time of the dance as a whole as created temporality and created time. Because time is not a thing which pre-exists and awaits carving up by the dancer, because it is something created by the dance itself, it exists specifically only in relation to a specific movement within the dance. The projectional quality which is part of the dynamic line, gives the dynamic line its temporal structure. The specific temporal flow of each movement is immediately apprehended with the created movement; thus, a specific degree of attenuation, of initial impulse and release, or of explosive thrust, is immediately intuited with the dynamic line.

If the dynamic line is the guiding thread in the development of the form, the temporal continuity of the dance will be apparent in the internally related projections of force. *Each movement, by virtue of its projectional quality, contains its own necessary temporal span of execution, by which it not only completes itself but prepares for the next movement.* This temporal relationship of one movement to another was implicitly described in the previous chapter: the dynamic line of a dance is the spatially unified and *temporally continuous* flow of force which is the sheer form-in-the-making. It may be recalled that to develop the dynamic line logically means to develop movement according to the context and accrued import of all previous movement. It is therefore apparent that the end of any movement is both end and preparation. There is no illogical jump from one movement to another. For example, if the arm is abducted and adducted, the end of the abductive movement is also a preparation for the adductive movement. It is in the context of what is immediately present and all that has gone before that movement is developed from the immediate present.

Hence, the projectional quality controls the temporal flow of a movement and the temporal flow is an integral part of the dynamic line; to designate the dynamic line of a movement as Bah!, BAAAAAAAAAAAAAAAA, or Bah, is to specify a particular temporal flow. We must now look to the other qualities of force to determine in what way they affect this temporal flow.

Phenomenologically, to move is to change qualitative relationships. Because a new movement changes one or all of the preceding qualities of force, it affects the dynamic line. For example, to turn the head from a straight forward position to the side in the context of a dance will affect the dynamic line, not only in terms of the way in which force is projected, but also in terms of the changing linear design of the body, the changing tensional quality, etc. Similarly, to jump into a crouched position is not only to affect the dynamic line in terms of the manner in which the jump is executed, but also in terms of the changing areal, linear, and tensional qualities. Any new movement will perforce alter at least one quality, and it may alter all of them. When one movement has been completed, it can go no further; a change must be made, a new movement created. But because each new movement arises from the conditions set forth by the preceding one, because the end of any movement is *both end and preparation*, the change is an internal nexus binding one movement to another. Each qualitative aspect of the present movement contains within itself its future quality. Because the new grows out of the old, because movement is not merely superadded, change relates to the internally regulated qualitative flow of movement.

The flow is not a monotone of movement, but a dynamic interplay of forces which rise and fall, recoil and expand, which have sudden shifts in direction, which are now vigorous, now flaccid, and so on. This very interplay of forces describes the qualitative interrelationships within movement, the changes which make the flow dynamic. If the dynamic line of the movement is vocalized, these changes are clearly delineated, for it is obvious that a new movement is the creation of a new dynamic line, or better, the further development of a dynamic line. Dance is composed of movements which continuously change previous qualitative definitions. To move in any way from where one is, is to change positions, and this changing of positions is a continuous occurrence in dance. What is immediately apparent is that each change has, by its very qualitative definition, a unique intensity, a unique impact. It has a certain potency according to its tensional quality, but also according to the manner in which, and the extent to which, the change is made. Thus, not only do the varying tensional qualities within the dynamic line provide gradations in intensity by changes in the potency of force, but also *any change in linear, areal, or projectional quality* creates varying degrees of intensity. Any change in direction, any change of shape, any change in the way force is projected will create, aside from or in addition to changes in tensional quality, a unique intensity of force; the flow of force, the line, by its very qualitative definition, becomes dynamic.

It is phenomenologically evident that each successive movement creates a qualitative change, and this, in turn, creates an accentual pattern, changing intensities, within the dynamic line. For example, in the context of a dance, a simple quarter turn

from a straight forward position to the side will have a specific
intensity because the turn is a new movement, and the new
movement is a qualitative change . The turn may vary all
immediately previous qualitative definitions: the tensional quality may change from limp to vigorous; the linear design of the
body may change from a vertical line to a vertical-horizontal line
as the turn is made; the areal design of the body may change
from an expansive to a contractive shape as the turn is made; the
projectional quality may change from what was perhaps an
abrupt movement forward to a sustained movement in the turn.
The linear and areal patterns perforce change with the turning
movement itself, because the direction of force is altered, and
the shape of the created space is further qualified. The intensity
of the turn, the impact it has, may be anywhere from weak to
strong depending upon the qualitative changes made, which
qualities are held constant, and the manner and extent to which
others are varied. The beginning of each movement, therefore,
creates a unique accent, not in the sense that the beginning of
each movement is necessarily stressed, but in the sense that it
marks off, by its very change, a new revelation of force: there is
not only a new temporal flow, but a new temporal-qualitative
flow.

The intensities within the dynamic line of movement are
controlled by all the qualities of force. It may be asked, then,
how the vocalized dynamic line, which presumably may only
reflect the intensity of tensional and projectional qualities, may
also reflect a linear and areal intensity as well. This question is
related to a previous question about the vocalized dynamic line
and is answerable in a similar manner: the vocalized line reflects
a particular spatialization of force. Because it immediately
reflects the inherent spatiality of the dynamic line of the
movement, it reflects any *change* in the linear and areal qualities
of movement; hence, it reflects the intensities created by the
linear and areal qualities, the impact of any particular spatialization of force.

Each new movement, each revelation of force, creates a new dynamic line such that each movement is, in fact, actually a change in all the qualities, even if some are held constant, as, for example, no variation in the projection of force, no change in tensional quality, and so on. Because the "constants" inhere in a new qualitative configuration, because there has been a change, of whatever minor order, there is a new movement, and thus a new dynamic line. Moreover, because no quality exists apart from the other qualities, because movement synthesizes all of them, the vocalized dynamic line cannot but reflect the total qualitative structure of the movement: any change in any quality will be intuited as a dynamic shift of emphasis. For example, consider vocalizing the dynamic line of two quarter turns: the beginning of each turn, *the mere change in direction and shape*, will initiate a new dynamic line. There is a vocalization of each turn as a distinct linear-areal change, quite apart from any other qualitative changes which might be present. Intensities are created by change, change in any or all of the qualities of force. One may thus speak of spatial and temporal intensities as well as the more common tensional intensities, that is, the impact of the forces themselves. All are inherent in the dynamic line of movement, and all are reflected in the vocalized line.

Each revelation of force is thus a phenomenon which presents a qualitative as well as temporal structure, and this temporal-qualitative structure is the dynamic line. When we intuit the dynamic line, we intuit the temporal-qualitative interrelationships of movment, the interplay of changing temporalities and changing qualitative intensities inherent in the perpetual revelation of force. If the dancer is implicitly aware of the dynamic line, she intuitively grasps the peculiar and unique temporalities and shifts in intensity inherent in the movement. She may also vocalize the line apart from the movement to become explicitly aware of the dynamic interplay of forces.

It might certainly be questioned how anyone can talk about

dynamic line, time, or accentual pattern in dance and ignore the fact that movement actually does have relative temporal and accentual values. One can answer this question first by saying that to intuit a dance is to be oblivious of duration or stress per se; an audience does not count or seek out the meter of movements being performed, and neither is it involved in assessing the relative stress values of the movements. Yet although the audience is seeing a dance and not a series of movements, it is evident that something can be said about why dance appears as it does.

We may first of all look back to the phenomenological description of dance as the creation of an illusion of force, an illusion which creates its own time and space. Time and space are not containers in which dance occurs; they are intrinsic dimensions of the illusion, virtual force, and as such, they are immediately created with the creation of that force. Further, as we have seen, the time and space of the dance are a synthesized totality of past-present-future, and not a succession of points or moments. But what of the dancer creating the form? She is at times certainly aware of, and in fact, commonly seeks out, a definitive structure: this dance is in 4/4 time; this interval of movement is twice as long as the previous interval; this movement is heavily stressed, and the next three are progressively weaker; etc. There is a counting out, a measurement of time and a measurement of stress:

```
  ′              *              *   *
  1 & 2 & 3 & 4 & / 1 & 2 & 3 & 4 &              ′—light accent
  ___ __ _____    _ _ ___ _____               *—heavy accent
```

Such a definitive structure is a rhythmic structure: it stipulates the relative duration and stress of each movement and thus gives a particular kind of knowledge about movement. The measurement is not and cannot be absolute because not only are the designations "heavy" and "light" ambiguous, but so also is the duration of each interval. The ambiguity derives from the fact that there is no way in which an absolute stress value or an absolute tempo may be indicated, with the exception of a metronome in relation to tempo. The accent may only be suggested by the use of relative terms such as "heavy" and "light," and the tempo by "slow" and "fast." Further, since the duration of the intervals is ultimately a function of the tempo, durations are likewise relative. The rhythmic structure is thus subordinate to the dynamic line inasmuch as the dynamic line does indicate an absolute tempo, duration, and accent; the tempo, durations, and accentual patterns within the dynamic line are absolute because the dynamic line is the movement: this unique flow of force and none other. It is therefore readily apparent that although rhythmic structure is inherent in movement, it is inherent in movement *qua* movement. It is not an immediately intuited phenomenon, but a phenomenon which demands reflection in order to be known. That rhythm in dance derives from reflective knowledge about movement is immediately apparent in the fact that the moment rhythm is pre-reflectively experienced, it ceases to exist for us: phenomenologically, there is no longer an awareness of duration, tempo, or stress apart from the dynamic flow of force itself.

The difference between the rhythmic structure of movement and the dynamic flow of force which is the dance, may be more fully clarified by an example. It is not uncommon for one to be captivated by, or experience the excitement of a particular flow of force. When one sees or hears such a flow, what is intuited is not a series of counts with appropriate accents,

```
 *   *   *     *   *   *   *   *   *       * *
 1 2 3 4 5 6 / 1 2 3 4 5 6 / 1 2 3 4 5 6 / 1 2 3 4 5 6
 ― ― ――― ― ― ―  ― ― ――― ― ―――
```

but rather, a dynamic flow of force in which the temporal and accentual changes constitute the very flow itself. What intrigues us is not how long a specific interval endures, but how it flows from and into other intervals; not how much an interval is accented, but how the total flow is inspirited by changes in intensity. Analogously in terms of the performing dancer: although the meter, the accents, the temporal values of the movements themselves, denote a precise yet relative rhythmic structure, the dance does not come alive until the dancer passes beyond a mastery of the structure, and comes to realize the dynamic flow inherent in the total piece.

To divide a dance into a series of longer, shorter intervals, intervals of greater and lesser stress, is actually to notate movement and not dance, for dance does not exist as a series of moments or points. Yet to assess relative temporal-accentual values, to count out durations of time and points of stress, is of vast importance in dance: to notate a dance, to facilitate recall of past dances, to teach a dance to others, all these practical considerations necessitate an exact reflective knowledge of the rhythmic structure. A dynamic line is as elusive as the dance itself; it exists only insofar as the dance is being created or presented, formed or performed. There is no way to record a dynamic line except perhaps by filming the dance. Consequently, to analyze the movement apart from the dance does not mean that the dance may not be created or re-created; it means only that the rhythmic structure of the movement, the mere series of movements, is to be taken as a concrete guide to the creation or re-creation of the dynamic line; and the creation or re-creation of the dynamic line will result in the creation or re-creation of the dance. Thus, one might begin composing a dance by outlining a specific rhythmic structure, according to which movement is subsequently created. But the dance does not exist until the specific structure becomes a felt flow of force, until the peculiar and unique intricacies of its qualitative and temporal shifts are intuited dynamically, *until the mere series of movements becomes a dynamic flow of force.*

Rhythm may thus be predicated of movement, but not of dance. Only movement as the actual stuff of which dance is made has a rhythmic structure; dance, strictly speaking, does not. Rhythm cannot be equated with dynamic line both because it is a quantitative structure explicitly known, and also because it cannot in any way reflect the created space of dance; it can in no way indicate the spatialization of force as the dynamic line does. For example, if a movement were designated as,

the head rotating from an original centered position to the left, right, left, right, left, it is clear that the movement is neither created nor experienced as a form-in-the-making, but as a means of arrival at a specified place by a specified time. In effect, it is not spatial designs and patterns inherent in movement as a revelation of force which are engendered in a rhythmic pattern of movement, but spatial positions arrived at; and it is obvious that spatial positions arrived at are not only objective realities, but realities which tend to be static. As such, they are almost the antithesis of movement: an emphasis upon spatial placement by-passes the very movement itself, the movement being no more than a means of realizing specific, predetermined spatial ends. Explicit knowledge of spatial positions in dance is of unquestionable importance in learning or notating a dance; the choreographer-dancer must be able to discriminate precise spatial relationships and positions in terms of a metric sequence. But such reflective knowledge does not constitute the dance. A rhythmic structure is basically a reduction of movement to its tensional and projectional *components* alone; it cannot capture nor be affected by the total qualitative structure of movement as a revelation of force, the structure which is the foundation of dance.

In view of the above discussion, a distinction may be made between a reflective awareness of rhythmic structure on the one hand, and dynamic line on the other. The former is a practical tool whose value lies in its practical application; the importance of the latter is aesthetic. The one gives knowledge about a series

of movements, the other about a unified and continuous form.[1]
The dynamic line of movement is created by the unique
interrelationship of all of the qualities of virtual force: a sheer
force of whatever potency spatializes and temporalizes itself in a
particular manner, and in so doing, it creates changing temporalities and changing intensities which uniquely characterize the
dynamic line; hence, a particular form-in-the-making is created
and presented. The qualitative basis of the temporalization of
force has thus been fully explicated. What must follow is a
description of the qualitative structures inherent in the spatial
flow of movement as a revelation of force.

1. See Susanne Langer's parallel account of rhythm in music (*Philosophy in a New Key*, New York, 1948, p. 196). Rhythm in dance
is analogous to "temporal measure" in music; dynamic line in dance is
analogous to "musical rhythm." The latter ". . . results from the internal,
tonal organization of the motif."

CHAPTER IX

THE IMAGINATIVE SPACE
OF DANCE

The imaginative space of dance is its created space. The created space has to do primarily with the imaginative moving visual forms created by the linear and areal qualities of movement as a revelation of force. In order to describe these forms, we must first clarify what is meant by the term "image" in reference to body movement and distinguish it from the total body image construct. The imaginative space of dance concerns only the mental image or picture of the body and the body in movement, and not the body schema through which we apprehend the moving spatial presence of our bodies. The bodily schema processes, as will be evident, are extrinsic to the image although knowledge emanating from these processes supports the creation of the image. In its general neurophysiological-neuropsychological sense, body image usually subsumes not only body schema, but body percept and body concept as well. To obviate confusion, we shall distinguish the characteristics of a mental image, the imaginative representation of an object through a visual-kinetic form. The approach is phenomenological rather than scientific; the concern is with the nature and appearance of the image itself, and not with its neurological stratification. The following description of the nature of an image is based upon Sartre's phenomenological account of its characteristics.[1]

The key characteristic of a mental image is that it is a representation of an object which is absent. In perception, we encounter an actual object, whereas on an imaginative level, we synthetically create the object. The imaginative consciousness, like the perceptual, conceptual, or affective consciousness, is a particular mode of the global consciousness. Each mode is a unique kind of conscious functioning.

Secondly, in perception, an object has many relationships to other things, an infinity of appearances. An imaginal object, on the other hand, has but one immediate and absolute appearance; it is an intentional object of consciousness, constituted by consciousness itself. Thus, one's knowledge concerning the imaginal object is also immediate and absolute, for nothing is to be found in the image except what consciousness intends. It is not a question of learning something from the image, for no new knowledge can accrue from it.

Thirdly, the object of the image is posited as not being present, as not existing, as existing elsewhere, or its actuality is not posited at all. The object of the image is, in other words, intended and constituted as an unreal object. If body movement is the object of the image, then body movement will appear imaginatively as a form, having no actual existence. This negation will become clear as we proceed to describe the imaginative representation of the body and the body in movement.

Finally, the image is an immediate and active representation.

1. Sartre, *The Psychology of Imagination* (New York, 1948), pp. 3–21.

It appears the moment it is intended, fully and wholly. It is not formed piecemeal; any attempt to compose an image additively results in a series of unique and absolute images.

In relation to these four phenomenological characteristics of a mental image, how does consciousness apprehend movement imaginatively? The very intention of consciousness to apprehend movement imaginatively means that movement will constitute the object of an image, and that it will appear as an imaginative visual-kinetic form. The imaginative form may be linear, and, in fact, movement is commonly apprehended as a linear form, a trajectory, such as the flight of a golf ball, which does not actually exist. Movement may appear as flight, depending upon whether the person is perceiving the movement or apprehending it imaginatively. Thus, one may perceive the moving ball or imaginatively apprehend the flight, the trajectory created by the moving ball. In the latter situation, the trajectory which the movement creates is posited as not actually existing in order that it may be constituted imaginatively by consciousness. It is constituted not as a series of images, but as a unified and continuous image. So long as consciousness intends the movement imaginatively, the image appears as a unified and continuous visual-kinetic form, and knowledge of the movement as a specific visual-kinetic form, such as a parabolic curve, is given with the image itself.

Consciousness apprehends movement imaginatively in apprehending imaginative forms created by movement. For example, movement as a revelation of force is always directed along linear paths; hence, imaginative linear patterns are always created by movement. Yet since these patterns do not actually exist, they may only be apprehended by an imaginative consciousness. To speak of any spatial forms in dance, shapes as well as curves, diagonals, verticalities, etc., is to speak of the imaginative visual-kinetic forms immediately created by movement: they are not only linear forms but areal forms as well. They relate to the created space of dance which appears the moment movement is created and apprehended not as actual movement, but as a revelation of force. If movement is intuited as a revelation of force, the linear and areal qualities of force will necessarily constitute a part of the intuition. The imaginative awareness of linear and areal qualities is part of the direct and immediate awareness of the total and perpetual revelation of force; it does not exist as a separate intuition or apart from the intuition of the dance itself, but is intrinsically related to the whole—in the same way that the qualities themselves exist within the total illusion of force and have no existence apart from that global phenomenon.

It is thus immediately apparent that neither the temporal nor peculiarly spatial moments of these forms actually exist apart from their conformance within the total structure of the illusion. To speak of a linear form, for example, is to abstract one of the peculiarly spatial moments from the total structure of the illusion of force for the purpose of analyzing the phenomenon of force. Furthermore, since there is no spatiality without temporality and no temporality without spatiality, the peculiarly spatial forms are really spatial-temporal forms: they are always unified *and continuous*. The linear pattern is not a series of discrete spatial points apparent *in time*, and neither is it a unified spatial image *in time*. The linear pattern is a unified and continuous image because it is a structural form existing within the total structure of the illusion of force, whose spatiality and temporality are not reducible to units of space and units of time. Its spatiality and temporality exist because the total illusion of force exists.

A linear visual-kinetic form may serve to illustrate further the intrinsically imaginative nature of movement and the inseparability of its spatial-temporal structure. To say that a dancer is moving in a circle means that we, as audience, are imaginatively apprehending the movement as a visual-kinetic form, a circle, which does not in fact exist. The circle does not exist except as it is imaginatively constituted by consciousness as a unified and continuous form, except insofar as there is a retentional knowledge of the circle as it is being drawn. We form an imaginative *Gestalt* of the movement by apprehending each moment of the circle as a spatial-temporal present in relation to a spatial-temporal past and future: the present is a flight out of the past toward a future. It is a transitory moment of an imaginative spatial-temporal whole and not an isolated present. Consequently, there is not a succession of images but a single and unbroken circular line.

Although it is clearly apparent that consciousness apprehends movement in dance imaginatively the moment movement is intuited as a revelation of force, one may question how it is possible to apprehend a circular path, for example, without being specifically aware of the actual movement which describes that path. To the extent that one is interested in exploring and clarifying a perceptual-imaginative relationship, one will ultimately note the relationship of the bodily schema processes to the imaginative consciousness of movement. In terms of a phenomenological analysis, the appearance of the imaginative visual-kinetic forms is proof enough of their existence within the total structure of the illusion; as human beings, we are all capable of apprehending linear patterns, or any imaginative visual-kinetic forms created by movement in dance, and the appearance of these forms may be described. Nevertheless, some observations may be made concerning the status of the actual kinesthetic or visual impressions in relation to these forms.

Sartre has spoken of the kinesthetic impressions as being actual and concrete.[2] They allow the imaginative visual form to be present to conciousness, and thus allow the form to attain a quasi-visual reality: if one envisions a circle and moves in such a way as to describe the circle, the circle attains a quasi-visual reality. The movement is guided by the actual and concrete

2. Sartre, *The Psychology of Imagination*, p. 111.

kinesthetic impressions, and these, in turn, support the creation and apprehension of the imaginative circle.

Since Sartre views perception and imagination as two mutually exclusive modes of consciousness, however, the kinesthetic or visual impressions as direct perceptions cannot exist concurrently with the image. The image is not a directly sensible phenomenon, but rather, an imaginative visual-kinetic representation. Therefore, one cannot presume that the kinesthetic or visual impression exists as a subliminal perception because its actuality and concreteness would allow it to be discriminated. We will therefore look more closely at the perceptual-imaginative relationship and suggest an alternative meaning of "actual" and "concrete."

One of the many interesting examples which may illustrate the validity of the question is tracing a circle with the fingertips while keeping the eyes closed. This example, of course, illustrates the question from the dancer's point of view, the dancer being usually unaware of her movement visually; hence, the concern with kinesthetic rather than visual impressions in relation to the imaginative consciousness of movement. How does the dancer know that she has completed the circle, and how does she know that her movement has actually traced the imaginative circle? It is immediately apparent that answers to these questions are founded upon the inherent spatiality of consciousness-body and thus, upon the bodily schema.

The dancer has a fund of lived experiences of her body in movement, and consequently, a highly developed pre-reflective awareness of the moving spatial presence of her body. She is capable of performing many movements which non-dancers could not perform without a reflective awareness of their bodies. The dancer *implicitly* knows that she has completed the circle and that her movement has actually traced the imaginative circle, because past experiences with her body exert their influence in the form of knowledge through the bodily schema upon any present condition. A spontaneous shift occurs from the imaginative mode to the perceptual mode automatically upon completion of the circle. The shift occurs at the moment the beginning point of the circle is reached: there is no need to corroborate the position of the fingers with the circle at various points as the circle is being drawn. The actual movement which will describe the circle is already known. The pattern for the movement is already a part of the global bodily schema. The kinesthetic impressions are therefore actual and concrete not in relation to the image, but in relation to the pattern projected by the bodily schema: they are extrinsic to the imaginative consciousness of movement.

A more comprehensive answer might be given by considering the nature of the kinesthetic impressions and the nature of the image. The image is unified and continuous because it is intended and constituted by consciousness. The kinesthetic impressions are made to be continuous and unified by the bodily schema processes. Without this integrating structure, the impressions would exist as seriate impressions. If an imaginative circle is to be traced by actual movement, the circle exists as an imaginative *Gestalt*. The kinesthetic impressions accompanying the movement are therefore actual and concrete, not in the sense that they are perceived, but in the sense that they are integrated with the bodily schema; and their integration aims at and guides the movement toward a realization of the imaginative *Gestalt*. It is consequently the actuality and concreteness of kinesthetic *knowledge* which is of concern, for it is the kinesthetic knowledge, and not the kinesthetic impressions per se, which actively guides the creation of the imaginative visual-kinetic form. Impressions are related to other impressions and not to the image because the image does not and cannot exist serially; it cannot be constituted on a point to point basis without a new image being created at every point. The interrelationship of the impressions is the basis of knowledge about the actual movement. Such knowledge guides the dancer as she moves along the imaginative circle. The dancer *implicitly* knows the meaning of her movement through the bodily schema; the kinesthetic impressions are meaningful immediately and directly because the pattern of movement is projected as a *Gestalt* upon the bodily schema. Knowledge of the actual movement is thus implicit and supports the imaginative visual-kinetic form. But knowledge of the actual movement is extrinsic to the imaginative visual-kinetic form: only knowledge of the imaginative form, that is, knowledge of the form *as a circle*, is intrinsic to the form.

It therefore becomes clear that it is not a question at all of a perceptual-imaginative relationship, for as long as consciousness intends an imaginary object, it will not perceive actual movement. It is rather a question of how knowledge of the actual movement supports the imaginative visual-kinetic form. To answer this question fully, it is necessary to consider the inherent spatiality of consciousness-body, the implicit awareness one has of one's moving spatial presence through the bodily schema. The question, "How does the dancer know?" is really "How does the dancer *implicitly* know?" and the answer might be given, "In the same way a blind man 'sees' with the tip of his cane." The purpose of this discussion, however, has not been to provide a comprehensive answer, but to illustrate the scope of the original question, How does consciousness apprehend movement imaginatively?; and to affirm that any answer to that question must be founded upon the inherent spatiality of consciousness-body.

We have seen that it is within the nature of movement itself to be imaginative, that imaginative visual-kinetic forms are created by movement, and that within the context of dance, these forms have to do with the created space of dance. We may now proceed to describe the appearance of all the imaginative visual-kinetic forms in dance. The imaginary lines created by movement, the linear patterns of force, have been dealt with almost exclusively only in order to keep consistent the illustrations of the intrinsically imaginative nature of movement, and the imaginative consciousness of movement.

There are four ways in which the spatialization of force in dance appears as an imaginative visual-kinetic form: (1) it appears as a linear design, as an imaginary line being drawn along the length of all body parts, effecting a directional configuration of the body as a whole; (2) it appears as a linear pattern, as a pre-existing imaginary line which the movement traces, or as an imaginary line being drawn by the movement; (3) it appears as an areal design, as a unified but ever-changing three-dimensional shape; (4) it appears as an areal pattern, as the shape of the space created by movement.

If the object of the image is the body itself, what is presented is an image in the form of a line representing the linear design of the body as a center of force. It is a moving image, for the imaginative line representing the body does not pre-exist imaginatively to be filled in by the body, although presumably one could "step into" a pre-existing imaginative linear design. Most commonly, the body is imagined as being drawn, and the drawing exists in the form of an imaginative line which moves out the length of the body parts to form a complete imaginative visual configuration of the body as a whole. For example, if the dancer is in an upright position, her awareness of the linear design of her body is in the form of an imaginary line extending the length of her body, from her heels to her head or vice versa. The line is, in effect, the imaginative vertical linear design which her body creates. It may be recalled that to describe the linear design of the body as being vertical is not to describe the body as a static object. The verticality of the body describes a dynamic positional configuration, a continuous directional projection of force; hence, it is clear why these imaginative forms have been described as visual-*kinetic* forms. The inherent kinetic structure of these forms may in fact be illustrated further: if the dancer is in an upright position with the arms extended to the side at shoulder height, she may be imaginatively aware of the linear design of her body as a cross, first the vertical line being drawn, then the horizontal, or vice versa. The significant point is that the line of force is imaginatively *drawn:* the dancer cannot apprehend the cross of her body all at once without creating an image of a static cross in front of herself, thereby disassociating herself from the dynamic linear design of her body.

What the dancer creates for herself imaginatively exists equally for the audience. The audience is not aware of the dancer's body as an actual body, but as a center of force which presents changing linear designs. Thus, the audience does not see an actual body in an upright position with arms extended to the side at shoulder height, but sees the linear design, that is, the cross, created by the body as a center of force. The linear design is an apparent quality of movement when movement is created and presented as a revelation of force. However, the particular linear quality which constitutes the appearance of the cross in no way constitutes the total movement. It is only one quality of the whole. It may be emphasized again, furthermore, that the qualities cannot be put together separately to add up to the whole which the movement presents. The quality of the whole is different from the sum of the qualities which constitute its apparent parts. The linear design is part of the total and immediate revelation of force. Moreover, it is clear that it is but one of many dynamic forms existing within the total dynamic form of the dance. It is abstracted from the total dynamic form in order that its appearance may be described, in and of itself. But this description of its appearance exists only within the context of the total illusion of force from which it has been abstracted.

From a description of the linear design of the body, we may proceed to describe the linear pattern of body movement. Linear pattern is an intrinsic quality of movement as a revelation of force. The pattern may be either a pre-existing imaginary line which the movement traces, or an imaginary line which is drawn by the movement. When a line "pre-exists," it does so through the phenomenon of focus. Insofar as focus is an intended but undrawn line, it may pre-exist as a line of force which the dancer's movement may follow or trace. For example, a diagonal line may pre-exist imaginatively from the dancer's eyes to their directional point of contact. That line is a quasi-real visual-kinetic form which her movement will describe. Whether the linear pattern is traced or whether it is drawn by the movement, it is always an extension from a beginning point, for a directional line, a trajectory, is always present in movement as a revelation of force. Any movement whatever may be made, and an awareness of it will include an awareness of a specific linear form, for example, a circle, a zigzag, a scallop, a straight line. So long as dancer and audience alike are aware of movement as a revelation of force, linear pattern will constitute a part of that awareness.

Although we will note the significance of the imaginative space of dance in relation to composition in the following chapter, it may be mentioned here that since the trajectory of movement describes a linear pattern, the linear pattern of a dance may be abstracted from the dance as a whole and drawn graphically on paper. It may thus serve as a guide in the teaching of specific dances by representing the linear paths of force which the movement is to create. Such a representation is usually and necessarily limited to the directional path of the total moving body, whether parts of the body are moving concurrently or not.

The third imaginative visual-kinetic form which body movement creates is areal design. As a center of force, the dancer apprehends the areal design of her body imaginatively; areal design constitutes the imaginative shape of her body as a center of force. It is apprehended as a spatially unified three-dimensional mass which continuously changes its design. For example, in extending her arms to the side in the context of a dance, the dancer is imaginatively aware of her *total* body as a spatially unified three-dimensional mass which is expanding its spatiality, its areal amplitude. The dancer is not aware of her arms as existing separately from the rest of her body; she is not aware of the movement of her arms as existing apart from the rest of her body; nor, finally, is she aware of each dimension of her body as separate, as a distinct frontal, sagittal, and transverse plane. The dancer is imaginatively aware of the shapes which she, as a center of force, creates. The total body is therefore imaginatively apprehended as a shape, or better, as a spatially unified three-dimensional mass creating itself in various shapes. The created space of dance is again apparent, for the ever-changing shape of the center of force is a continuous spatialization of force, a continuously dynamic creation of imaginative visual-kinetic forms.

Just as the dancer imaginatively apprehends the areal design of her body as a spatially unified three-dimensional mass creating imaginative forms, so the audience imaginatively apprehends the areal design of the dancer's body. To use the above example, the audience is aware neither of the dancer's arms as existing separately from the rest of her body; of the movement of the arms as existing apart from the total body; nor of each dimension of the body as a separate dimension. The audience imaginatively apprehends the body as a center of force which is a spatially unified three-dimensional mass, a totality, which, by continuously changing its spatial amplitude, creates changing areal designs.

The areal design of the body is an imaginative visual-kinetic form which does not actually exist. What does actually exist is the human body, its parts—torso, arms, head, legs—and the shape it assumes as an actual body. The areal design is an imaginative representation of the total three-dimensional shape of the body as a center of force. But in contrast to linear design which may be described in terms of specific linear forms—diagonals, curves, and the like—areal design may not be described in terms of specific areal forms because there is no vocabulary which may communicate these ever-changing, dynamic, three-dimensional forms. The description of areal design must be limited to a description of the body as a center of force which spatializes itself; and this spatialization, in turn, may only be described in terms of the amplitude, the "expansiveness" or "contractiveness," of the center of force. The significant point in relation to the imaginative space of dance is that areal designs are not actual designs, but imaginative visual-kinetic forms created by the body as a center of force.

Areal pattern presents much the same difficulty as areal design in that its description is likewise limited: the amplitude of the created space of dance is "intensive" to "extensive." The areal pattern of movement in dance is the imaginative three-dimensional shape of the space created by movement. For the dancer as for the audience, the shape of the dance space does not actually exist but is imaginatively apprehended. If the shape of a dance could be sculptured, the sculptural form would represent the imaginative areal pattern of the dance. It would represent the amplitude of force, the extent to which force spatializes itself. Areal pattern, then, is similar to linear pattern in that it is intrinsic to movement: it is within the very nature of movement to create imaginative visual-kinetic forms, according to its amplitude as well as its direction.

The imaginative space of movement is intrinsically related to virtual force. It has to do with the spatialization of that force, the created space of any dance. Through an imaginative consciousness of movement, we are aware of the ways in which virtual force spatializes itself. Again, it may be noted that this is not a separate awareness, but part of the total and immediate awareness of the illusion of force. It is not a question of our putting something into the dance which is not already there. Linear and areal designs are created with the dance because the body of the dancer appears as a center of force. Likewise, linear and areal patterns are created with the dance because movement of that body appears as a revelation of force. These imaginative visual-kinetic forms are intrinsic to the total dance: they are structures inherent in the global phenomenon of the illusion.

Further, they are an ever-unified and ever-continuous creation: each linear and areal quality has a beginning and an ending, but an ending which germinates a new beginning. In the same way that a temporal flow exists by virtue of the fact that any movement, through its projectional quality, contains its own necessary temporal span of execution by which it not only completes itself, but prepares for the next movement, so a spatial flow exists by virtue of the fact that linear and areal qualities engender their own necessary spatial span of execution, by which they not only complete themselves, but prepare for a future quality. The basis for the spatial flow of force in dance is thus the unreal, yet clearly apparent designs and patterns which are internally related to one another, which appear as a unified and continuous creation, and which are integral parts of the total pure dynamic flow of force which is the dance.

In Chapter VII, it was stated that the spatialization of force has to do not only with the manner in which space is created but with the projected designs and patterns as well. Yet nothing thus far has been said of the manner in which space is created. Although it is neither a primary structure of movement as a revelation of force, nor a sub-structure of the linear and areal qualities of force, it is clearly a structure within the total imaginative space of the dance. Hence, its description has been delayed until this more appropriate place.

Phenomenologically, any projection of force creates a particular kind of space by the very manner in which it is projected and by the very nature of the force itself. If force is projected vigorously and abruptly, it may be apprehended as cutting through a resistant or opposing space; if projected in a delicate and sustained manner, it may be apprehended as gliding through a pliant or supple space; if projected in a ballistic fashion, it may be apprehended as thrusting through a resilient or buoyant space. In short, a spatial *texture* becomes apparent: the created space of dance has a textural aspect according to the manner in which it is created. As the above examples show, there are, very generally, three types of spatial textures: resistant, pliant, and resilient. It is obvious, however, that there is no absolute relationship of these textures to specific tensional and projectional qualities. A ballistic movement, for example, may create a pliant space, even a vacuum of space by ending in a collapse, just as a sustained movement may create a resistant space by pushing outward. Furthermore, within the context of any dance, there is no one spatial texture but perpetually changing textures, just as there are changing projections of force, and so on. What may certainly emerge, however, is a pervasive textural motif.

In terms of the projection of force itself, the nature of the created space may be more specifically described as resisting the projection of force, as opening easily to the projection, or as reacting to the projection. While one may speak of a created texture in terms of the projection of force, it is clearly apparent that space is not already there waiting to be made resistant, pliant, or reactive by the projection. The space itself is created with the projection and does not exist apart from the projection. It is thus that texture is a sub-quality within the qualitative projection of force, a sub-structure or sub-quality of movement as a revelation of force. Any projection of force creates its own time by the manner of its projection, yet duration is not a primary quality of movement as a revelation of force, but rather a structure founded in the projectional and tensional qualities of movement. In the same way, any projection of force creates its own space by the manner of its projection, yet texture is not a primary quality of movement as a revelation of force, but rather a structure founded in the projectional and tensional qualities of movement. Although it is immediately created and presented in any revelation of force, and although it may be analyzed as a created spatial structure in its own right, it may not be described apart from the projectional and tensional qualities which constitute it, and which are the essential substance of its existence.

Texture qualifies the created space of dance: the imaginative visual-kinetic forms created by movement, and the dance as a whole. As spatial designs and patterns are created, so are textures created which may intensify aspects of those designs and patterns. For example, in extending the arms up and forward in front of the body from an initially compact and vertical design, one creates a texture which may uniquely characterize the imaginative space of the movement by making aspects of it more prominent: the upward line of the movement may be emphasized if the projection of force creates a resistant space, or the expanding areal design of the body may be emphasized if the arms levitate, if they move as if without weight, effort, or support, thus creating a fluid, yielding space. Spatial textures are therefore similar to focus in that they can accentuate in one way or another aspects within the total spatialization of force, and are thereby integral parts of the imaginative space of dance. But unlike focus, spatial textures are not intrinsically linear nor do they emerge from intended but undrawn projections of force; they originate in, and are made apparent by the projections of force themselves. Yet, as the above examples make clear, the manner in which space is created is not simply describable in terms of the tensional and projectional qualities themselves, but in terms of the unique resultant interaction of tensional and projectional qualities as they make apparent a particular spatialization of force. Texture results from this qualitative interplay.

Texture may also qualify the imaginative space of the dance as a whole, if a dominant textural motif emerges. Thus, the total created space may appear as a viscous density, an underwater realm, which is resistant yet yielding; it may appear exciting and resonant, a thoroughly reactive and volatile space; it may appear obstructive and adverse, an almost impenetrable space; and so on. Whatever the textural motif of the dance might be, that motif characterizes the spatiality of the dance and is an integral part of the total illusion which the dance creates.

Through the preceding descriptions of the qualitative structures inherent in the temporal and spatial flow of force, the nature of the created form of dance has been fully explicated. Further, it has become clear how the created form comes to be in and of itself expressive of a pure phenomenon of feeling. Movement as a perpetual revelation of sheer force creates a dynamic organization on the basis of its qualitative structure, and this dynamic organization, this interplay of sheer forces, reflects a pure phenomenon of feeling. A specific dance creates a highly individualized flow of virtual force in terms of the sheer forces themselves, and also in terms of the unique temporality and unique spatiality created by the forces. When the spatial-temporal structures are abstracted from the total illusion of force, they may be described not only in relation to the flow of force itself, its *ekstatic* and diasporatic nature, but also in relation to the qualities of force through which they are made apparent: tensional, linear, areal, and projectional qualities. When the qualities are thus abstracted from the total illusion of force, we see why each dance creates a highly individualized flow of force and a highly individualized expressive meaning: the qualitative interrelationships describe a unique dynamic line. The particular tensional, linear, areal, and projectional qualities of movement as a perpetual revelation of sheer force, together create a particular dynamic organization of force. The dynamic structure of the dance as a whole, its unique interplay of fluid, ever-changing forces, is the foundation of its import.

The descriptive elaboration of dance as a uniquely created and uniquely appearing phenomenal presence has been fully realized in the analysis of the intrinsic nature and phenomenological structures of the total illusion of force. It is on the basis of this analysis that we may now attempt to pinpoint the educational implications of a phenomenological approach to dance.

CHAPTER X

EDUCATIONAL IMPLICATIONS:

DANCE COMPOSITION

In order to compose, the dancer must think in movement. An idea expressed in words does not constitute the beginning of a dance. Although it may certainly serve as impetus for a dance, an idea must be transformed into movement, for a dance is movement and only movement from beginning to end. Elementary? Yet there are ways of teaching dance composition which by-pass the truth of such a notion, partly because the clear-cut distinction between what is commonly called a "dance study" and a dance composition is often only superficially maintained, perhaps because a lucid description of the basis for the distinction is lacking.

A dance study is an incomplete symbolic form. It lacks a formal fullness and depth to be completely expressive in and of itself. It does not formally reflect the pure phenomenon of any feeling in that its form is not sufficiently elaborated to be expressive of any feeling. In short, a dance study lacks the wholeness necessary to a full-fledged symbol. A dance composition, on the other hand, is a symbol, a complete form needing no further elaboration. It stands in and of itself as a concrete work of art.

It is pertinent to explore this distinction on the basis of dance being "movement and only movement." If the student in a composition class is asked to do a "study in line," or a "study in theme and variations," for example, it should be clarified that she is working with movement and only movement *qua* movement, and only incidentally or accidently with movement as a perpetual revelation of force, and thus, with the inherent dynamic line of movement. A "study in line" exemplifies those studies in which a component of actual movement is abstracted from the total structure of movement. A "study in theme and variations" exemplifies those studies in which an abstract concept is to be "put into" movement. In the former situation, actual components of movement are abstracted from movement as a whole, singled out for study; in the latter, structural elements of form are abstracted from a hypothetical, ideally ordered form.

In working with an actual component of movement, the dancer will of necessity be working with all the components of movement because movement synthesizes all components. But the apparent totality of movement is incidental to her particular purpose, which is to do a study in *line*. Similarly, when the dancer works with a structural element of form, other elements will be apparent, or they may be recognized as lacking, but the apparent order of the form as a totality is again incidental to her purpose, which is to do a study in *theme and variations*. Thus, not only are movement and form considered separately, but also the very nature of a study separates a particular aspect of movement or form the totality of movement, or form. Dance studies thus involve an abstraction of movement from form or

form from movement, and a further abstraction of a particular
component of movement from actual movement or of a particular element of form from an ideal total form.

We may point out the dubious value of a study in which
structural elements of form are singled out by reiterating what
was said of these structural elements in the chapter on abstraction: they exist either as abstract concepts or as abstracted
elements of an already completed form. But furthermore, an
abstraction of form from movement can never be wholly successful, for the student must work at achieving her "theme and
variations" in movement. She must transpose the idea "theme"
into movement theme—a particular kind of projection of force,
a particular line of focus, etc. The movement, as such, is still not
created as a particular revelation of force, but as a particular kind
of movement. The emphasis in the end is always upon movement *demonstrating* a particular kind of formal element, and a
consequent limiting of its appearance to that element.

It is apparent, then, that what is lacking in a study to give it
the fullness of a dance is precisely the wholeness and plasticity
which may only be achieved by abstracting movement from its
symptomatic or referential context in everyday life, and by
abstracting the form of human feeling from its actual affective
context. As noted previously, both these abstractions are made
simultaneously: movement does not exist apart from form nor
does form exist apart from movement. Any attempt to separate
the two must be recognized as an artificial separation for the
purpose of describing their phenomenological structure in relation to the total phenomenal presence of dance. Thus, a study is
not only an unrealized symbol because of the concentration
upon movement as actual movement; it is also an unrealized
symbol because of the inherent limitations which it poses; that
is, it lacks both an abstraction from everyday life and the
consequent plasticity which comes from such abstraction, and
abstraction and plasticity are intrinsic characteristics of a created
movement form, a dance. While abstraction is inherent in both

a dance study and a dance composition, it is what is abstracted which elucidates the foundational distinction between them. A study is always ultimately a study of some abstracted aspect of movement, even if it concerns a structural element of form, as noted above. The purpose of the study is to explore the particular abstracted aspect as a concrete thing in itself. Hence, by its intrinsic limitation, the study delimits movement to be known as one particular thing, both as it is created and as it is presented: if a "study in line" does not, in fact, revolve about linear designs and patterns, it fails to be what it sets out to be or is required to be.

On the basis of the foregoing distinctions, one may ask what the value of a dance study is. The delimiting nature of a study gives the student the opportunity of pushing beyond her present creative range by seeking out and discovering new movement. Yet beyond this immediately apparent value, a second and equally important value emerges. Because the student's attention is focused upon a single component of movement, and because the development of movement revolves about that component, the student may become sensitive to the way in which that component of movement affects the other components. For example, in a study in line, the student may discover how a circular linear pattern influences the areal component of movement: the largeness or smallness of the circle is contingent upon the direction of movement at all points along the circle. Similarly, the student may discover how the manner in which she moves affects the continuity of the circle: an even, sustained projection of movement will create a continuous circular line, whereas an uneven, abrupt and sustained projection, will create a discontinuous line. The dance study, in delimiting movement to be known as one particular thing, affords the student the opportunity of discovering how the components of movement are mutually affective. By working with a separate component of movement, the student can increase her sensitivity to the way in which that component immediately creates the other components. Because she is not working with movement as a totality, the discerning student may discover how movement is perforce a totality the moment it is created: she will recognize that in creating a single component of movement, she is creating all components.

If the distinction between a dance study and a dance composition is kept clearly in mind, it is possible to recognize and affirm the overall value of a dance study: it prepares the student for dance, and thus comes under the heading of technique rather than composition. Technique is never anything more than a preparation for dance, and creating dance studies is a particular kind of technique. It prepares the student for dance by allowing her to explore the actual components of movement in depth and thus increase her sensitivity to them and to their interrelationship. Dance studies are exploratory "forms" having to do with the exploration of movement as actual movement. A study in abrupt movement, for example, allows the student to become more familiar with the possibilities of movement within the specified limitation, and more aware of how any particular abrupt movement will immediately create and affect all other components.

If dance studies afford the opportunity of exploring the actual components of movement and are vital to the student's scope and understanding of movement, they cannot be a means to teaching students about composition. The question then remains: How does one teach dance composition? Insofar as such a question implies that one can teach people how to compose, as if an infallible recipe existed, dance composition cannot be taught. One can only offer the student the opportunity of gaining insight into the nature of dance as an illusion of force by working with movement as a revelation of force; hence, *working with movement as sheer appearance*, which means abstracting movement from daily life as the symptomatic or referential expression of feeling, and *creating it as a dynamic form-in-the-making*. The student will thus gain insight into the temporal and spatial structures inherent in that form, and insight into the qualitative structure, the dynamics, which particularize that form and make it unique.

The dynamic line characterizes the qualitative inter-relationships of a movement form; the way that form flows and the way in which its flow is marked by changes in qualitative intensities. The dynamic line, as it is reflected upon, thus comes closest to pinpointing the lived experience of the dynamic movement form. The lived experience of the dynamic move-ment form is the immediate experience of an illusion of force which is always moving: it is always dynamically flowing to a spatial-temporal future. The sheer appearance of force, the illusion of force, is a sheer appearance of dynamics. An aware-ness of the dynamic line which any movement form creates is therefore an awareness of an illusion of force, whether this awareness is pre-reflective or reflective. So long as what is reflected upon is still movement as a dynamic form-in-the-making, and not actual movement, the illusion of force does not capitulate or disappear upon reflection. Consequently, whether the dancer is pre-reflectively or reflectively aware of the dynamic line as she composes, she will be aware of a sheer flow of force.

But how, one may ask, does one specifically lead students to an awareness of the inherent dynamic line of movement? First, as noted above, by allowing them to work with movement as a dynamic form-in-the-making. For example, a simple movement phrase might be presented: extending the arms overhead as one lunges forward on the right foot, adducting the arms to the side as one makes a quarter turn to the left and shifts his weight to the left foot, and extending the arms overhead again as one raises the right leg flexed at the knee. Each student would use this plastic movement phrase as a point of departure. The dynamic flow which each student would create in working with the *total* movement phrase would necessarily be the focal point of awareness: the simplicity of the movement would obviate any preoccupation with parts of the body or aspects of the total movement. The movement would be created by each student as *sheer movement*. And each student would thereby realize its plasticity, its freedom to be whatever she wishes to make it. How each student organizes the movement will determine its dynamic structure. For example, a student might lunge forward abruptly and strongly, execute the turn in a weak, sustained manner, give a sharp initial impulse in raising the leg and arms, and continue the movement in a weak, sustained manner. After the students work with this simple phrase to their satisfaction and create a specific dynamic organization, they may then vocalize the dynamic line which they have created in order to test their sensitivity to the dynamic organization. Their ability to achieve an exact verbal rendering of the dynamics of the movement form will assure their grasp of those dynamics.

In such a situation, it is apparent that the students would be working with movement as a totality and as a revelation of force; they would be working neither with separate aspects of movement, nor with movement as a symptomatic or referential expression of feeling. Each dynamic form-in-the-making would be a potential dance. Each would be a potential dance because each is a sheer form of movement which creates a beginning illusion of force. Moreover, it is obvious that each beginning illusion is unique because each dynamic structure is unique. In order to develop any sheer form further, the student must be aware of its unique dynamic flow to that point. To give a gross example, if the student has created the form in a lyric manner, and if she is aware of the dynamic flow inherent in that beginning lyric form, she will not develop the form further by stamping several times, clapping her hands overhead, then falling to the floor while at the same time contracting and expanding the areal design of her body. The specific flow of force which she has created germinates a specific development. In order to realize a unity and continuity in the development of the form, the student must never lose her sensitivity to the dynamic line inherent in the sheer form of movement she has created: its suspensions, its intensities, its propulsions, and so on. It is, after all, the coherency and flow of the dynamic organization which makes the form in and of itself expressive of a pure phenomenon of feeling. Without this coherency and flow, the form cannot achieve a significant expression. The student, therefore, must always be aware of the way in which the form pulsates. And she may test and reinforce such awareness through a vocalization of the dynamic line she has created.

It is possible to illustrate further the way in which one might specifically lead students to an awareness of the inherent dynamic flow of movement: the same movement phrase might be used in many ways by the same student, to the end that a variety of dynamic organizations are created on the basis of a single and constant movement phrase. The student may thus become more sensitive to the vast number of intricate shadings possible in the creation of a dynamic line. To use the previous example, the student may discern the difference apparent in the dynamic line when she shifts her weight to the left foot upon completion of the turn, and when she shifts her weight to the left foot as she turns; indeed, she may become aware of the shadings possible in the dynamic line according to how far she shifts her weight to the left. The movement phrase is an unformed movement idea which becomes a specific, dynamic form-in-the-making as soon as it is created. The student may use the same unformed movement idea to create a variety of specific, dynamic forms, and thus increase her sensitivity to the nuances of movement which affect the dynamics of the form. She does not reflect upon the movement before she moves, *but has the lived experience of the movement first.* The dynamic form-in-the-making exists only because the dancer has moved. The dancer is immediately and implicitly aware of the unique dynamics of the form-in-the-making as she creates it. She may vocalize the dynamic flow to reinforce her awareness of the dynamics as she moves, and she may also vocalize the dynamic line after moving in order to reflect upon the qualitative intricacies of that flow.

The dancer, as she is composing, must continuously evaluate the form which she is creating. The problem of critical evaluation in dance is apparent in that the dancer cannot get outside herself to see the dance as she is creating it. It is therefore vital that the dancer be made aware of concrete means of evaluating her own dance as she is composing it. The critical viewpoint is a reflective viewpoint, but it cannot be a reflective viewpoint unless the dancer first *lives* the form she is creating, and unless she knows what to criticize; that is, what she is working toward. If she is working toward a unity and continuity of form which will, as a totality, be symbolically expressive, then what she will criticize will be the unity and continuity of that form. The unity and continuity of the form which she criticizes is, in fact, her own pre-reflective awareness of the form. Her intuition of the form as she creates it is the basis for her reflective judgments upon that form. Again it is emphatically clear that the experience must be had before it can be reflected upon or judged in any way. *Hence, the prime importance of the pre-reflective awareness of sheer movement which is an awareness of a dynamic form-in-the-making.* If the dancer in composing is unaware of movement as a dynamic totality, and is instead reflecting upon aspects, actual components of movement, she will never realize a unified and complete movement form, and her reflective judgments upon the movement form will be, in reality, reflective judgments upon segments of it. In short, the dancer will never be able to reflect upon the unity and continuity of the movement form as a whole, in all its vibrancy and fullness, unless she is first pre-reflectively aware of that movement form.

The pre-reflective awareness of the body in movement as a dynamic form-in-the-making is inherent in any lived experience of sheer body movement. It is not a special kind of awareness which must be cultivated, or which only a select few may achieve. One must only stop reflecting—analyzing, interpreting, judging—long enough to grasp it. When the dancer does grasp her body in movement as a dynamic form-in-the-making, she has the foundational awareness requisite to an informed and meaningful reflective criticism of dance. What becomes essential in teaching composition, therefore, is constant emphasis upon the lived experience of sheer movement.

Once the student has the total lived experience, once she is aware of the dynamic interplay of forces in the very creation of those forces, she may go on to consider their inherent structures; for example, the imaginative visual-kinetic forms created in any projection of force. The significance of these forms will become apparent as they are related to the total form of dance which she is creating. If the dancer has started a composition and has developed the form-in-the-making according to the dynamic line it creates, and if she is at an impasse to go any further, no matter how intently she tries to grasp the future of the dynamic line, she may reflectively look back at the composition in relation to the imaginative forms she has created: she may look more acutely at the spatialization of force, abstract it from the total flow. She may become aware of the kinds of linear patterns she has created, the linear designs of her body as a center of force, and so on. A reflective awareness of these forms may help her to develop the total form further by allowing her to contemplate the spatialization of force to that point, the space which she has thus far created.

We may illustrate this reflective awareness of spatial forms by recalling the example of how a student might have organized the plastic movement phrase: lunging forward abruptly and strongly, executing the turn in a weak, sustained manner, giving a sharp initial impulse in raising the leg and arms, and continuing the movement in a weak, sustained manner. If this movement phrase constituted the beginning form of a dance, and if the student was unable to develop the form further through her awareness of its dynamic line, she might reflect upon the specific visual-kinetic forms inherent in the structure of that line. She might reflect, for instance, upon the particular diagonal line her body projected in the lunge; whether its direction was more vertical than horizontal; whether her arms were an elongation of the diagonal line, or whether they were vertical; the extensiveness of the lunge; the expansiveness of the arm gesture in the turn; the extent to which the leg was raised from the floor; whether her focus was straight ahead at all times, or whether it shifted up, down, or to the side; if within these designs and patterns a textural motif was apparent; and so on. The particular spatial forms are abstracted from the total form the student has created. In reflecting upon them, the student may discover that she has spatialized force in a generally expansive manner, that the movement has an "outward" spatial quality. She may discover that the linear quality of her movement has been primarily vertical: that there has been no sequential movement to break the upright line of her torso, that the directional quality of the total movement phrase has a vertical emphasis. Finally, she may discover that the created space has a germinal fluid texture. Such reflective knowledge of the beginning form may help the student to develop the form further through an explicit awareness of the spatial unity of the form, its spatial flow, to that point.

Similarly, the dancer may look back more acutely at the temporalization of force, the tensional-projectional quality of the form. Thus, she may become reflectively aware of temporal-qualitative patterns, such as the way in which an abrupt movement is followed by a sustained movement, even the way in which the breath is sharply inhaled and slowly exhaled. The student may specifically reflect upon the abruptness of her lunge forward, its temporal span of execution, and the way in which it flows into the slow, sustained turn. She may consider whether the temporal span of the abrupt lunge is brief, and the turn projected immediately after, or whether the body is "held" briefly after the lunge before beginning the turn; whether the abruptness of the lunge creates an incisive beginning; to what degree the turn is sustained; the way in which the turn flows into the succeeding movement, whether it is simply a continuation of the turn or whether there is a momentary "stop" before the leg and arms are raised; the degree of sharpness in the initial impulse which initiates the last movement; to what degree the sharp initial impulse is separated temporally from the sustained raising of the leg and arms; and so on. All these temporal-qualitative patterns have to do with the way the student has projected force; hence, the unique *flow* of force she has created and the way that flow is marked by qualitative intensities. The student's reflective awareness of the manner in which she has temporalized force will allow her insight into the temporal continuity of the beginning form she has created; whether within that continuous flow there are definite breaks after each movement, or whether the temporal span of one movement spills over into the next. In brief, she will know the temporal span of each movement, the way in which it begins, the way in which it ends, the way in which its ending prepares for a new beginning, and the way in which the total flow of force is characterized by changes in intensity. An awareness of the dominant temporal-qualitative motifs which delineate the temporal continuity of the form may allow the student a clear realization of how the total form may be developed further.

Once the lived experience is had, once the student is able to apprehend her body in movement as a dynamic form-in-the-making, she may reflect upon the lived experience of that form in order to develop it further. The student's reflective awareness of the particular spatial-temporal structures she has created will give her insight into the particular qualitative interrelationships which constitute the dynamic line; she will, in other words, become aware of the structural basis of the dynamic line. In such reflective analysis the student realizes that her abstractions of qualities from the total flow of force are never anything more than abstractions: she realizes that she cannot actually look at linear and areal qualities apart from the projection of force which creates them; and similarly, she cannot actually look at the projection of force apart from the linear and areal qualities created by the projection. She realizes that temporality does not actually exist apart from spatiality nor spatiality apart from temporality, and that neither exists apart from the total illusion of force. Because the dancer has started with the total lived experience and not with isolated segments of it as given units, she realizes that what she looks at reflectively are aspects or structures of the whole, and structures which have no meaning apart from the whole. Consequently, she also realizes that she may not develop the form further by putting together the structures which she has isolated reflectively, for these may only serve as guides to the further development of the *total* illusion of force.

With these remarks it should be clear how a phenomenological approach to dance composition offers the student guides to composition on the basis of her own lived experience and consequent understanding of dance. What is "taught" and what is consequently created has nothing to do with movement as actual movement. One can assign a student to create a dance only insofar as that student has worked with or knows how to work with movement as sheer appearance, and hence, only insofar as the student is aware neither of her body nor of her body movement as an object or instrument, but rather, is aware of her body in movement as a dynamic form-in-the-making. The basis for a phenomenological approach to dance composition is the foundational structure of consciousness-body itself, the way in which consciousness lives its body in movement in everyday life as a form-in-the-making. In dance, this form is a sheer form. It is a lived experience of the *sheer phenomenon of movement,* virtual force, from beginning to end. It would seem imperative then that a class in dance composition center around this lived experience.

CHAPTER XI
EDUCATIONAL IMPLICATIONS:
DANCE AS ART

It was noted in the first chapter that dance is sometimes taught as a means to education. Yet in light of the descriptive study of dance which has been presented, it would seem that education should be a means to dance, a means whereby its uniqueness and vitality would be concretely illuminated. To explore such a notion in fuller perspective, let us first examine briefly some of the current attitudes concerning education, and their relationship to dance.

In general, education is considered a means. Even if defined as a terminal process, as completing one's academic studies, it is still apparently a means to a further end outside itself: a means to productive living, to releasing the developmental potential within any given individual, to broadening and deepening an individual's span of interest, and so on; in brief, a means to many goals and objectives currently conceived to be the purposive ends of education. It is clear, then, that while educators are concerned primarily with *educational* goals, these goals can only be extrinsic to the educational process itself. But education cannot afford to be equivocal on this point: it cannot be both an end in itself and a means to an end beyond itself. If it could, the conception of any particular subject area within education would become nebulous and indeterminate, a mere function of what constitutes the end of education. Since all education concerns specific areas of study, it becomes vital to determine first how education relates to the particular field of study which is of concern, and secondly, how the ends of education, whatever they might be, are realized through education within the same area.

This first clarification is no less vital than the last: if dance is taught as a means to education, which is itself a means, then any inherent value dance might have is doubly removed from the center of attention it deserves; if dance is taught as a means to education as end, then what is dance education other than the learning of skills, facts, and the like about dance? Surely what one would call "real" or effective education is not concerned with a knowledge or reiteration of facts, or with the acquisition of certain specified abilities: education does have recognized goals beyond its own inherent process, goals which have something to do with the way in which an individual develops and relates to the world.

Likewise, it has become increasingly more apparent that if the value of dance is made to coincide with the extrinsic ends of education, such ends come to govern the educational approach to dance; that is, the way in which dance is defined, and the way in which it is presented and evaluated. The approach derives from what is agreed upon beforehand as being an educational goal, and dance is sifted, as it were, through an educational sieve, so that what is taught will coincide with the predetermined end. In effect, what dance is, is in practice what the educational goals make it.

To overlook the labor and vital engagement necessary to the creation of a dance, and to concentrate instead on effective group interaction, individual growth, self-realization, or whatever might come from such creation, is actually to nullify the dance. And not only for the individual composer, but also for the people who see it: not in the sense that something called "dance" is not present to the audience, but in the sense that what the audience sees may not be dance. And if it is not there in the first place, it is questionable whether the audience will look at it and evaluate it in terms of educational aims. Perhaps the audience has seen an earlier work and can say that the choreographer has matured in her creative abilities, but that is all they can say. It is the dance, the very created work itself, which is overlooked.

For the student of dance, the consequence is the same and yet more personal: the essential purpose of her labor and creative efforts in composing or learning a dance is grossly minimized. Further, when the concentration is on the student's social, intellectual, or emotional development, the student suffers because what she thinks she is doing is not what she is actually doing; and evaluations following performance—even critical reviews—will bring her deficiencies to light. In sum, to consider dance as an educational means creates, in practice, a dichotomy which need not exist between any phase of development and dance since, in fact, individual growth or self-realization need not be measured by anything other than the success of the dance itself.

If we begin by accepting not dance, but education as a means, and a means to something outside itself, not only do we confront the issue with no prior valuational determinations, but we also confront the basic question which the issue engenders; namely, what is the value and place of dance in education, and how does dance as subject matter relate to the achievement of the extrinsic ends of education? That dance as art is not in and of itself coincident with the extrinsic ends of education is obvious, for dance is not in and of itself a means to individual growth, self-realization, productive living, or what have you; it is an aesthetic activity. That it is and should be an end in itself, therefore, may become obvious if one takes into account people's keen interest and appreciation of it, and if one is thereby led to discover the intrinsic values which are the foundation of such interest and appreciation. Moreover, if the ends of education are outside itself, the educational value of dance could well be dance itself.

If we look at dance from the composer's viewpoint, it is clear that there is nothing which is non-educational about creating a dance: it is a total engagement of the individual in which he perforce encounters himself in depth, in which he utilizes the fullness of his resources, in which he draws upon his past experiences and knowledge, in which his discrimination and sensitivity to form are, in fact, tested as *creative intelligence*. Furthermore, the creation of a dance is necessarily connected with individual growth, self-realization, and the ability to work well with others, since it puts so much stress on something of recognized and paramount importance in the world, yet something which education does not often specifically state as its goal: communication.

If education is itself a means, it can and should be a means to *enlightened creativity, performance, and criticism*. But if this is so, one must not embellish dance on the other end with predetermined values. Because the creation of a dance does engage the choreographer and dancer so wholly, because it undoubtedly contributes to individual growth and self-realization, the value of dance in education may be individual growth and self-realization, but of the dancer as dancer, and of the composer as choreographer. The value of dance is dance. It is a unique and vital communication which needs no further justification, whether professional or educational.

If the art of dance flourishes as a consequence of the emphasis upon the aesthetic nature of dance, there need be no concern about whether educational ends are being pursued, or whether dance is a fit subject matter for education: the realization of the ends of education is an almost inevitable consequence of the concentration upon the dance as dance, the dancer as dancer, and the composer as choreographer. And the reason is that the ends of education are by-products of the aesthetic activity. The dancer cannot create and continue creating, and remain at a standstill from an individual-growth point of view; the dancer cannot work with other dancers in composing a dance, and remain insensitive to good group relations; the choreographer cannot create and the dancer cannot perform the dance, and remain oblivious to an audience's critical reactions to the dance, such that nothing is learned from the creative and performing experiences.

In sum, the choreographer neither creates nor does the dancer perform in an introspective vacuum. The ends of education, while being extrinsic to both the creative and performing act, become apparent; they do not have to be forged onto dance-as-subject-matter prior to the creation and performance of dance. The realization of these ends is, in fact, contingent upon the realization of dance: the realization of dance as a formed and performed art is the concrete context within which growth and development occur. *Without creation, without performance, without insightful criticism, there is no context within which a developing awareness of self may occur, and consequently, no way of evaluating individual growth.* So long as the total concentration and emphasis is upon the creation, performance, and criticism of dance, the educational values of dance will emerge as meaningful, but peripheral, benefits from the primary aesthetic value of dance.

In light of the foregoing clarifications, it is possible to detail the implications of a phenomenological approach to dance. One of the first of these concerns the professional dancers whose very

arrival on the academic scene is an implicit affirmation that the
phenomenon of dance exists prior to a consideration of dance as
subject matter for education. But of equal significance is the fact
that a reverse exchange is not common: educators are rarely
sought by professional dancers or companies to give master
classes or to be educators in residence. And perhaps the reason
for this lack of a reverse exchange is that educators do not always
focus upon the fundamental phenomenon: dance, the formed
and performed art. If they did, education in dance would center
around the lived experience of dance regardless of the particular
area—teacher education, research, indeed, even professional
dance—in which they were teaching. Because educators are
primarily teachers of dance and not dancers, and because professional dancers are primarily dancers and not teachers, educators
might contribute significantly to the educational programs
within professional dance; they might enrich the programs not
only by their ability to teach, but also by the very scope of their
practical and aesthetic understanding of what it means to teach
dance. Thus, one of the educational implications of a phenomenological approach to dance is the possibility of a broader
and more meaningful exchange program between educators in
dance and professional dancers. It would seem that such a program could be mutually supportive and enlightening.

It was stated earlier that perhaps the reason why professional
dancers are already asked to teach in an educational program is
that something is lacking in "educational" dance. It was suggested that a phenomenological analysis of dance might lay the
groundwork for a distinction between movement education and
dance in education, and it has. In dance, movement as movement does not exist. In dance, movement appears as a revelation
of sheer force emanating from a body which appears as a center
of force. The difference between movement as objective movement and movement as a revelation of force is analogous to the
distinctions made between objective space-time and lived space-
time. Yet phenomenologically, an analysis of movement has

demonstrated that the inherent spatial and temporal structures of consciousness are foundational to *any* lived experience of movement; phenomenologically, one would begin with a description of the inherent spatiality and temporality of human consciousness-body whether one was describing movement or dance, because these structures are part of the total lived experience of any kinetic phenomenon. Thus, whether one is concerned with everyday movement, sports, or dance, the foundational structures of consciousness-body are part of the lived experience of the phenomenon. What differentiates dance from movement is that the lived form-in-the-making is created as a sheer form in and of itself, and unlike other movement activities, such as basketball, gymnastics, and the like, it has no meaning beyond itself.

Moreover, dance is created as a sheer form which is symbolic; hence, one which is abstracted, plastic, and expressive. Since it is created as a sheer symbolic form, dance creates and sustains an illusion of force. None of the structures within that sheer symbolic form, or illusion, are reducible to objective units of force, time, or space; and conversely, the sheer symbolic form is not merely the sum of its inherent non-objective structures. Movement, on the other hand, may be reduced and analyzed apart from the lived experience, as a functional unification of objectively determined space-time co-ordinates, and vector quantity of the actual force expended. This is true for the experience of movement in everyday life, including sport activities, and for other physical achievements with objective ends. Dance is only analyzable in relation to the lived experience of the total structure of the illusion of force and cannot be objectively reduced to extrinsic ends.

On the basis of the foregoing discussions of the place and value of dance in education, of the potential interaction and intercommunication between dance-educators and dance-artists, and of the distinctions between dance and movement, an overall educational implication of a phenomenological approach to dance becomes obvious: dance can be taught only as the formed and performed art that it is; to teach it as something else is, in effect, to teach something else. If students, as well as audiences at student concerts, are to have unique and vital, lived experiences of dance, the center of attention must be the thing itself—the phenomenon of dance as it is created and presented.

It is in connection with the creation and presentation of dance that a final point may be made concerning the educational implications of a phenomenological approach to dance. It was stated in Chapter II that dance is often defined as the expression, the evocation, or the communication of feeling, but that no clear description is given as to how dance functions as any one of these, if, in fact, it does at all. Through this phenomenological study of dance, it has become apparent that dance is not concerned with the expression of feeling in the sense of an actual sentient expression; it is concerned with the symbolic expression of feeling. The dance is not a symptom of the dancer's feelings, but a created form symbolic of the form of human feeling. Neither is dance concerned with the evocation of feeling in the sense of an actual sentient experience. The audience does not feel fear, jubilation, or whatever, but intuits the feeling symbolically expressed. The feeling is immediately reflected by the symbolic form: it is neither deduced from the form by the audience, nor is it attributed to the form as a consequence of a feeling it might have evoked in the audience.

Dance communicates feeling insofar as it achieves a complete symbolic form. What is simultaneously intuited by the audience is the form and the import of that form: the intuition of the dance is a unified and continuous intuition, just as the symbolic form and import of the dance are unified and continuous. Since dance is concerned with the communication of feeling through a symbolic form, the dancer, by the very nature of her work, has what might be called a social obligation: to make clear the *form* of her expression so that it is *immediately* meaningful to others. It may be pointed out that the emphasis in a purely educational evaluation is therefore upon individual growth in a social context: the ability of the dancer to develop a form which does in fact communicate; which is, in its very presentation, a unique and vital experience for all concerned. To find the yardstick which would measure self-actualization, or any other designation for personality maturation, by itself, is at best hard to come by, and nearly impossible to isolate operationally. But a dance as a work of art, is either there or it is not. If dance itself is the criterion for dance in education, there is no possible equivocation.

The concern of the dancer must then be turned inside out in order to realize the communicative powers of dance. We may note first of all that novice dancers, especially, sometimes think that to dance means to express themselves. But aside from the misapprehension that dance is a form of self-expression, the concern with the body as a technical instrument must not lead to a *preoccupation* with flexibility, strength, kinesthetic awareness, co-ordination skills, and the like. A side to side movement of the rib cage, the ability to maintain a fifth position, the ability to extend the leg to waist level and hold it there—all these are technical proficiencies which may be mastered, but which have nothing to do with dance except insofar as they *prepare* the body for dance. *Each dance creates its own inimitable technique.*[1] There is no ready-made technique which one simply learns and then makes dances with. Any systematic preparation for dance, any technique, is a vital necessity, but should not be pursued as if it were an art in itself.

It may be noted that professional schools of dance seem often to overemphasize the technical training of the dancer to such an extent that technique does not seem a springboard for individual creative work, but an end in itself. The student, however, must pass beyond mere technical mastery, for it is only by forming and performing dance that a dancer's technique *develops:* the

1. See Collingwood: "Expression is an activity of which there can be no technique." (*The Principles of Art*, p. 111.)

technique of dance is ultimately *the ability to move according to the demands of the form being created or presented.* Hence, in order to realize dance as a unique form of communication, one must certainly not neglect or minimize the technical training necessary to a comprehensive preparation for dance, but one's ultimate concern must be with the phenomenon of dance, its creation and presentation, and not with the phenomenon of one's own body, except insofar as the latter is necessary to the former. Because communication is the province of dance, but a particular kind of communication, and one which necessitates a particular kind of technique—not merely in the sense of possessing specific skills or abilities, but more broadly in the sense of being able to meet the demands of the dance itself—the educative value of dance as dance clearly originates in the creation of dance itself.

To go back to dance, again and again, is to rediscover its uniqueness and vitality. In thus going back, in following the phenomenologist's prescription, we have found *dance as art.* If such a study has been profitable, it should provide the foundation for a vigorous, intensive, and continuing study of dance as a formed and performed art; and it should also provide the foundation for a re-evaluation of dance in education, and a consequent renaissance of the art of dance through education. This is the insight derived from the phenomenological approach to dance; any conceivable future benefits to dance as art or to education in the art of dance which would accrue to this descriptive analysis must wait upon practice within the classroom-studio.

BIBLIOGRAPHY

Cassirer, Ernst. *Philosophy of Symbolic Forms*. Ralph Manheim, trans. Vols. I and III, New Haven: Yale University Press, 1953.

Collingwood, R. G. *The Principles of Art*. Paperback reprint. New York: Oxford University Press, 1958.

Croce, Benedetto. *Aesthetic*. Rev. ed. Douglas Ainslie, trans. New York: Noonday Press, 1960.

Hawkins, Alma. *Modern Dance in Higher Education*. New York: Bureau of Publications, Teachers College, Columbia University, 1954.

Hayes, Elizabeth R. *Dance Composition and Production for High Schools and Colleges*. New York: Ronald Press, 1955.

H'Doubler, Margaret. *Dance: A Creative Art Experience*. 2d ed. Madison: University of Wisconsin Press, 1957. 1st ed. New York: F. S. Crofts & Co., 1940.

Humphrey, Doris. *The Art of Making Dances*. Barbara Pollack, ed. New York: Rinehart and Co., 1959. Paperback reprint. Madison: University of Wisconsin Press, 1962.

Jordan, Diana. *The Dance as Education*. London: Oxford University Press, 1938.

Kaelin, Eugene F. *An Existentialist Aesthetic*. Madison: University of Wisconsin Press, 1962.

Langer, Susanne K. *Feeling and Form*. New York: Charles Scribner's Sons, 1953.

————. *Philosophy in a New Key*. New York: New American Library, 1948.

————. *Problems of Art*. New York: Charles Scribner's Sons, 1957.

Melcer, Fannie Helen. *Staging the Dance*. Dubuque, Iowa: Wm. C. Brown Co., 1955.

Merleau-Ponty, Maurice. *Phénoménologie de la Perception*. Paris: Librairie Gallimard, 1945.

Radir, Ruth Anderson. *Modern Dance for the Youth of America*. New York: Barnes, 1944.

Russell, Joan. *Modern Dance in Education*. London: Macdonald and Evans Ltd., 1958.

Sartre, Jean-Paul. *Being and Nothingness*. Hazel Barnes, trans. New York: Philosophical Library, 1956.

————. *The Psychology of Imagination*. New York: Philosophical Library, 1948.

Thevenaz, Pierre. *What is Phenomenology?* James M. Edie, Charles Courtney, and Paul Brockelman, trans. Chicago: Quadrangle Books, 1962.

Turner, Margery J. *Modern Dance for High School and College*. New Jersey: Prentice-Hall, Inc., 1957.

visual-kinetic form, 114–16, 120–22

Lived experience: of dance, 3–5, 6, 8, 12, 13–14, 15, 21–22, 28–29, 32, 38, 47, 64–65, 83, 99, 134, 137–38, 140, 141, 148; of time, 15, 16–20, 25–26; of space, 15, 22–25, 25–26; of consciousness-body, 36, 37, 46–47

Logical flow, 55, 76; of dynamic line, 92–93, 95–96, 98, 103, 135–36

Mental image, 112; characteristics of, 113–14

Movement: vocabulary of, 54–56, 123–24; *qua* movement and as revelation of force, contrasted, 78, 79, 130, 147–48; specificity of, 80–81; imaginative consciousness of, 114–19. See also Revelation of force

Phenomenology, 10–13; relationship to dance, 13, 29; educational implications of phenomenological approach to dance, 29–31, 141, 146–51. See also Dance, phenomenal presence of

Principles of composition, 73. See also Form, structural elements of

Projectional quality, 50, 56–57, 75; and dynamic line, 88, 89–91, 92, 94–96, 128; and temporality, 101–3; and texture, 125–26, 127

Reflective awareness: of the body, 26–27; of the dance, 38–41, 44. See also Composition, and reflective awareness

Revelation of force, 41, 50–51, 57, 66, 70–71, 75–76; as foundation of expressive symbol, 80–81; and expressive nature of form, 82–83, 84–85; and dynamic line, 83, 87–89, 105, 106, 111, 128; and rhythm, 110; and imaginative consciousness of movement, 114–15, 121, 122, 124; and texture, 125, 126

Rhythmic structure, 107–111

Sensuous surface, 80, 81–82, 84

Spatiality: phenomenological space, 15, 22–28; spatial *ekstasis*, 25; diasporatic nature of, 26; objective, 27; spatial unity, 34–35, 36, 37–38, 39, 40–41, 42–43, 44, 47, 64, 86–87, 89, 103, 115, 125, 139

Technique, 133, 150–51

Temporality: phenomenological time, 15, 16–22; temporal *ekstasis*, 16–18, 20, 25, 26; original, 16–20; static, 18, 19, 20; diasporatic nature of, 18, 26; dynamic, 18–19, 20; psychic, 20; objective, 20–21; temporal continuity, 34–35, 36, 37–38, 39, 40–41, 42–43, 44, 47, 48, 64, 86–87, 89, 102–3, 115, 140

Tensional quality, 50, 51–52, 75; and dynamic line, 88, 90–91, 92, 94–96, 128; and texture, 125–26, 127

Texture, 125–27, 139

Virtual force, 33–34, 41–42, 78, 141; spatialization and temporalization of, 34, 42–44, 48; and audience, 38–39, 40,